ABOUT THE CENTER FOR CREATIVE LEADERSHIP

The Center for Creative Leadership is an international, nonprofit, educational institution whose mission is to advance the understanding, practice, and development of leadership for the benefit of society worldwide. Founded in Greensboro, North Carolina, in 1970 by the Smith Richardson Foundation Inc., the Center is today one of the largest institutions in the world focusing on leadership. In addition to locations in Greensboro; Colorado Springs, Colorado; San Diego, California; and Brussels, Belgium, the Center has an office in New York City and maintains relationships with more than twenty network associates and partners in the United States and abroad.

The Center conducts research, produces publications, and provides a variety of educational programs and products to leaders and organizations in the public, corporate, educational, and nonprofit sectors. Each year through its programs, it reaches more than twenty-seven thousand leaders and several thousand organizations worldwide. It also serves as a clearinghouse for ideas on leadership and creativity and regularly convenes conferences and colloquia by scholars and practitioners.

Examples of the Center's work include

Benchmarks®, a comprehensive, 360-degree assessment tool that helps middle to upper-middle managers and executives identify strengths and development needs.

Leadership Development Program (LDP)®, a five-day experience that enables middle- to upper-level managers and executives to enhance their leadership skills in a variety of organizational settings, improve their ability to develop employees, and achieve excellence in all aspects of their lives.

Ideas Into Action Guidebooks, twenty-four- to thirty-page publications that show practicing managers how to carry out specific developmental tasks or solve essential leadership problems.

For more information on the Center for Creative Leadership, call Client Services at (336) 545-2810, send an e-mail to info@leaders.ccl.org, or visit the Center's World Wide Web home page at http://www.ccl.org.

Funding for the Center for Creative Leadership comes primarily from tuition, sales of products and publications, royalties, and fees for service. The Center also seeks grants and donations from corporations, foundations, and individuals in support of its educational mission.

Center for
Creative Leadership

leadership. learning. life.

Russ S. Moxley

Leadership and Spirit

Breathing New Vitality and Energy into Individuals and Organizations

JOSSEY-BASS
A Wiley Company
www.josseybass.com

Center for
Creative Leadership

leadership. learning. life.

Published by

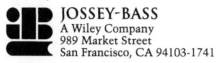 **JOSSEY-BASS**
A Wiley Company
989 Market Street
San Francisco, CA 94103-1741

www.josseybass.com

Copyright © 2000 by John Wiley & Sons, Inc.

Jossey-Bass is a registered trademark of John Wiley & Sons, Inc.

Jossey-Bass books and products are available through most bookstores. To contact Jossey-Bass directly, call (888) 378-2537, fax to (800) 605-2665, or visit our website at www.josseybass.com.

Substantial discounts on bulk quantities of Jossey-Bass books are available to corporations, professional associations, and other organizations. For details and discount information, contact the special sales department at Jossey-Bass.

Chapter 1 epigraphs: *The Age of Paradox* by Charles Handy. Copyright © 1994 by Harvard Business School Press. Reprinted by permission.
"The Killing Fields: Institutions and the Death of Our Spirits" by Diane Cory in *Insights on Leadership* edited by L. Spears. Copyright © 1998 by John Wiley & Sons, Inc. Reprinted by permission of John Wiley & Sons, Inc.
Chapter 2 epigraph: *The Practice of Management* by Peter F. Drucker. Copyright ©1954 by Peter F. Drucker. Copyright renewed © 1982 by Peter F. Drucker. Preface copyright © 1986 by Peter F. Drucker. Reprinted by permission of HarperCollins Publishers, Inc.
Chapter 3 epigraphs: *Spiritual Leading and Learning* by Peter Vaill. Copyright © 1998 by Jossey-Bass Inc., Publishers. Reprinted by permission.
"An Alternative to Hierarchy" by Gifford Pinchot. *Leader to Leader,* 1998, *10,* 43. Copyright © 1998 by Jossey-Bass Inc., Publishers. Reprinted by permission.
Chapter 4 epigraph: *Working* by Studs Turkel. Copyright © 1972 by Studs Turkel. Reprinted by permission of Donadio & Olson, Inc.

(continued on page 229)

We at Jossey-Bass strive to use the most environmentally sensitive paper stocks available to us. Our publications are printed on acid-free recycled stock whenever possible, and our paper always meets or exceeds minimum GPO and EPA requirements.

Library of Congress Cataloging-in-Publication Data

Moxley, Russ S., date.
    Leadership and spirit : breathing new vitality and energy into individuals and organizations / Russ S. Moxley.
        p.   cm.
    Includes bibliographical references and index.
    ISBN 0-7879-0949-1
    1. Leadership.   2. Industrial management.   3. Creative ability in business.   4. Organizational effectiveness.   I. Title.
    HD57.7 M69   1999
    658.4'092—dc21   99-6656

FIRST EDITION
HB Printing   10 9 8 7 6 5 4

A Joint Publication of

The Jossey-Bass Business & Management Series

and The Center for Creative Leadership

Contents

Dedicated to my mother,
PAT MOXLEY,
with gratitude for her great good spirit

Preface
A Story About This Book

It was seven or eight years ago that a brief conversation started me on a new leg of my life's journey and changed, at least in part, the focus of my work. The conversation brought up ideas that had been below the waterline of my thinking and perceiving but never come to the surface. The conversation happened at an unlikely time and with an unlikely person.

It was a casual conversation over lunch, not the place or time I expect to find deep insights. The person was Roland Nelson, an adjunct staff member at the Center for Creative Leadership (CCL), where I work. Roland had been president of two colleges in the earlier part of his career and was then on the faculty at the University of North Carolina at Greensboro. He also worked as an independent management consultant.

Almost as a side comment, Roland looked at the two of us sitting with him and said, "The most important dimension of leadership is one that those of us who work here are not willing to talk about."

Curious, I bit: "What's that, Roland?"

"It's the spiritual dimension," he said. As soon as the words were spoken, I knew they were true.

For almost thirty years, I have done management development, leadership development, and organization development work in a variety of organizations and in all sectors of the economy—private, public, and independent. Over the years, I have had the privilege of working with thousands of managers and executives to help them and the organizations of which they were a part of learn, grow, and change. As one part of this work, I have focused on helping individuals link their heads, hearts, and hands—to integrate thoughts, feelings, and behaviors. I thought that when they and I integrated these three dimensions of ourselves that have been so long divided, we would find the wholeness we sought. This was my on-the-surface understanding of wholeness.

The conversation with Roland helped me realize that this equation for wholeness wasn't complete. Since then, I have read different types of books and participated in new types of personal and professional development experiences. I have surfaced and written about "below the waterline" ideas in my journal, had deeper conversations with friends and colleagues and clients, observed new realities in the organizations in which I work, seen different dynamics in relationships, and looked at practices of leadership through a new lens.

What I now deeply believe is that we are more than a collection and integration of our thoughts, feelings, and behaviors. We are also spiritual men and women. Spirit is as much a part of us as are those other three dimensions, and it is just as natural as them. Spirit saturates and weaves through all of our experiences—those internal to us, and those that are external—and offers us a source of vitality not available from mental, emotional, or physical energy. Our journey toward wholeness requires that we learn to appreciate and integrate all four of these energies; our understanding and practice of leadership is incomplete unless it includes the use of all four.

I did not come to these beliefs quickly or easily. By personality, preference, and temperament, I prefer data and truth that can be known though one or more of my senses. I am logical and rational. But slowly and over time, as I reflected on my own experience and paid attention to the experience of others, I have come to believe that there are truths that cannot be empirically proven, truths about effective leadership that we have too long ignored. One of those truths is that our practice of leadership either suffocates or elevates spirit.

This book is my attempt to put on paper what I have learned.

Several years ago, I heard Peter Block say that he had good news and bad news about the research that provided the basis for one of his books. The good news was that it was based on a longitudinal study. The bad news was that it was based on an N (a number) of one. So it is with this book. The longitudinal study has spanned the thirty years I have engaged in my professional work—even longer if my early work experiences and educational experiences are included, experiences that were formative. But the N is still one. This book reflects what I have learned during those years. To be sure, along the way you will notice that I scatter in bits and pieces of data from others, and sometimes a story or two from others to help make a point. But this book is primarily a reflection of my growing awareness that spirit is a core dimension of the self; leadership and spirit are inextricably linked, for good or bad.

The Purpose of This Book

This book seeks to show *how leadership and spirit can be linked to promote new vitality and energy in individuals and organizations*. It is my hope that it helps you find new depth of meaning and satisfaction in your work, and in the leadership activities in which you participate. Doing this is not easy. As I try to make clear, linking leadership and spirit requires a new level of awareness and understanding—of ourselves, of others, and of the process of leadership—and the intentional development of new behaviors. But this is a way to make our work worth the investment of our lives.

There are four beliefs underlying this purpose:

- By and large today, American workers are a dispirited lot. Too many of us leave work each day feeling drained, deenergized, used up. As a result, we and our organizations are losing a source of vitality that is desperately needed.

- One reason we are dispirited is because of how leadership is understood and practiced. Too often, practices of leadership suffocate spirit. We can, and must, do better.

- There is a process of leadership that is inspiriting, a process that includes all of us, at different times and in different ways, in the activity of leadership.

- For this process to work, we must learn to be our true selves and our whole selves, and we must develop new ways of doing leadership. In short, we must *be* and *do* differently.

The Structure of the Book

The structure of *Leadership and Spirit* reflects these core beliefs.

The first part, Chapters One to Four, shows why leadership and spirit must be woven together. In Chapter One, I introduce "Composite Corporation" as a story of how and why employees become dispirited because of how leadership is practiced. The threads of leadership and spirit are first woven together in this chapter. The second chapter defines spirit and describes the way it works within us and among us. In Chapter Three, I describe and analyze prevalent practices of leadership, emphasizing those that cause spirit to wither and wane. The final chapter in this first part offers a different way of understanding and practicing leadership, and it provides examples of how this practice looks in day-to-day leadership activities.

Part Two demonstrates why we—each of us—must use our whole self in the activity of leadership; it identifies the capacities we must develop if this different approach is to be used effectively. A core idea stressed throughout the second part is that it is not enough to add new leadership skills or techniques or models to our repertoire, which is what we often attempt to do in leadership development processes. Instead, a focus on our being and our spiritual development must accompany new ways of doing. Getting to know various dimensions of ourselves, including learning how to embrace our shadow, is the emphasis of Chapters Five and Six. Chapter Seven identifies several of the skills and behaviors that reflect and give voice to the true self and that add to our capacity to engage in the activity of leadership. Chapter Eight links leadership, spirit, and community, describing things we can do to foster community.

The final chapter is an Epilogue, a framing of the choices that we each must make to write the endings (as we would like them to turn out) of our individual and organizational stories.

The Audience

For whom is this book intended? It is for men and women who have invested much of their lives in their careers, who have by and large been successful (at least as we usually define success), and who have discovered somewhere along the way that something is missing—that their careers, which promised so much, now appear at the very least somewhat hollow. It is meant for men and women in organizations who want more from work than a paycheck, who are prepared to invest themselves fully in their work, and who know that there must be a way to be a leader and do leadership that encourages the investment of our whole selves and best selves. It is written for workers, supervisors, managers, and executives who hunger for a better way.

In a larger sense, *Leadership and Spirit* is written for all of us. I make this bold claim because all of us will, during the course of our lives and careers, have opportunities to engage in leadership activities. Parents, teachers, youth workers (and youths themselves), service delivery providers, knowledge workers, widget makers, and those in formal management positions all engage, at least at times, in the activity of leadership. This book is written for all who want to lead fuller and more satisfying lives at work; it is offered with a belief that one way we can do this is to weave together leadership and spirit.

I received some confirmation of this claim from my wife, Jean, a gifted teacher who knows that teaching is her calling. Though the book is not specifically written for teachers, as Jean read each chapter of the draft she talked with me about how she could apply the concepts and practices in her classroom and more broadly in her school.

I hope that you, like Jean, can find useful ideas and concepts that you can apply, practices that will make the places where we work worthy of the time and energy we invest in them.

Acknowledgments

This book was not written by me alone. Along the path I've traveled in the past thirty years, I have had special teachers who challenged me, encouraged me, expanded my way of thinking and doing. You will find their fingerprints scattered throughout this book. Here I mention but four of the primary ones; there have been many others.

Through workshops, conversations, and his books, Peter Block was one of the first teachers to give me a glimpse of how leadership—or, in his words, stewardship—and spirit could be linked to bring new vitality to individuals and organizations.

Early in my journey, Peter Vaill, now the Distinguished Chair in Management Education at St. Thomas University, came to CCL to engage several of us in a dialogue about integrating leadership and spirit. His thinking was, and is, provocative and helpful.

I remember when I first read the introduction to James Autry's *Love and Profit* (1991). I was moved by it, and then by the rest of the book. Since then, I have been privileged to get to know Jim and learn with and from him.

More recently, I have learned from the writings of Parker Palmer. I've read and reread his books. His description of the inner journey has left me more willing to go on my own, and from his writings I have clarified my understanding of the link between inner life and outer work.

To these four teachers, I give grateful thanks for their insights and courage.

Several colleagues at the Center for Creative Leadership have taken parts of this journey with me. For the past several years, Robert Burnside, Meena Wilson, Kim Kanaga, Paige Bauswell, and Jessica Crawford have cohosted with me an annual conference on spirit and leadership. I have learned from each of them (and from those who joined us at the conference). Though their language is different from mine, the CCL's Wilfred Drath and Chuck Palus have done seminal thinking about new ways of understanding and practicing leadership, and I have learned from their conceptualizations. Martin Wilcox and Marcia Horowitz are editors at the center, and they have extended steady and needed encouragement. To these colleagues, heartfelt thanks.

One colleague at the center, Paige Bauswell, provided special help in the preparation of the manuscript. She edited the final draft, she demonstrated superb investigative skills as she searched for citations, she helped secure necessary permissions, she covered the office with patience and grace while I was writing. And she did it with skill and good humor. Thanks Paige.

Though I did not expect it, each person who reviewed the initial manuscript of this book identified himself or herself to me. Each gave generously of time and talent to help me clarify and strengthen ideas, and each provided needed support and encouragement. To Mary Lynn Pulley, Mike Murray, Richard Smith, and Peter Vaill, my deep gratitude. And I thank Byron Schneider, Dawn Kilgore, and Thomas Finnegan, the editors at Jossey-Bass with whom I worked, for their careful guidance, their ability to give feedback honestly and kindly, and their steady affirmations. This book is better—ideas presented more clearly and understandably—because of their work. In each of these relationships, I experienced the clear and present reality of spirit.

I have been graced through the years with friends who have shared the story of their journey with me and listened to mine. I think it is fair to say that we have grown together. To Richard Smith again, Virginia Duncan, Mike Murray, Peggy Cartner, George Peabody, Dan Pryor, Carole Hunter, Tim Rouse, Phyliss Hawkins, and Mignon Mazique, special thanks.

I also thank Matt and Ann and all the folks at Tate Street Coffee House in Greensboro, who offered me a space to reflect and write while I listened to good music and drank even better coffee. Tate Street has been my "downtown office" for the last five years.

These acknowledgments would not be complete without recognizing the special women in my life. I am surrounded by them: my mother, two sisters, four daughters, two stepdaughters, and Jean. These are women who engage life fully, each in her own way and with indomitable spirit. I am thankful for the spirit that is in each of them and that connects them to me. My life is fuller and more complete, and I am who I am, in large part because this is true. To each, my thanks and my love.

And a special word of appreciation once again to Jean, who gave me space and encouraged me while I wrote, who celebrated with me when ideas were working and listened to me when they weren't, and who always had confidence I could do it.

The Middle of the Story

When I started to write about leadership and spirit, I did it in a personal journal; my intent was simply to capture my musings. Later, as I was encouraged to turn my musings into a manuscript, I thought I would write about what I had learned over the years from my personal experiences in leadership activities and from working with others engaged in the same pursuit. I had learned, and now I would write—or so I thought.

I found instead that it was in the writing of this book that I learned. The very act of writing caused me to dig deeply, to consider again my inner life and my outer work. Intense reflections on my years of experience led me to uncover new meanings of those experiences. In the process of writing, I discovered new ways to synthesize ideas; out of the synthesis, old ideas were clarified and new ideas emerged. Even the struggle I had to communicate some of the ideas was growth producing.

Now, as I finish this book, there are parts I want to rewrite. Among other things, this tells me that I am continuing to learn. I realize that I am in the middle of this story. That's where you enter: in the middle of it. If I had the opportunity to hear your story, chances are I would learn something that I would want to add to this story. Because I cannot do that, I hope you will. As you read this book and consider your story, please add to this one so that together we can cocreate the ending we want.

Reading on, you will learn that if you join me in the act of cocreation you are, from my perspective, engaging with me in an act of leadership, an act that nurtures spirit.

The Author

Russ S. Moxley is a senior fellow and director at the Center for Creative Leadership, a nonprofit research and educational organization headquartered in Greensboro, North Carolina. As a senior fellow, Moxley focuses his time on executive coaching, executive team development experiences, and other leadership-development workshops in for-profit and nonprofit organizations, in the United States and abroad. He also works with organizations to help them put together leadership development systems.

He is coeditor and one of the authors of the *Center for Creative Leadership Handbook for Leadership Development* (Jossey-Bass, 1998). He is also the editor of the center's *Ideas into Action* guidebook series.

Outside CCL, he has been very involved in the Greensboro community, For several years, he cofacilitated the work of the Greensboro One Task Force and recently worked as a facilitator of another large citizen's advisory group that developed recommendations on the redistricting of the Guilford County Public Schools. He is an active volunteer with Habitat for Humanity and a member of Friends for Habitat.

Nationally, Moxley is on the governing board of the International Leadership Association and a member of the board of Spiritworks.

Before joining the CCL, Moxley worked for several years as manager of management and organization development for ARCO Alaska in Anchorage. He also served on the human resource development staff of ARCO Oil and Gas in Dallas. Prior to that he spent ten years as a principal in a training and consulting firm headquartered in Dallas.

Moxley received his bachelor's and master's degrees from Southern Methodist University in Dallas. Together, he and his wife, Jean, have six daughters.

Leadership and Spirit

Part One

Two Threads:
Leadership and Spirit

Chapter One

Weaving Together Leadership and Spirit

We are not destined to be empty raincoats,
nameless numbers on a payroll, role occupants, the
raw material of economics or sociology, statistics in
a government report. If that is to be its price,
economic progress is an empty promise. There
must be more to life than being a cog in someone
else's great machine, hurtling God knows where.
                    —*Charles Handy (1994, p. x)*

There is a lie that must be named and a truth that
must be told. Our institutions are killing our spirit.
We are allowing it to happen.
                    —*Diane Cory (1998, p. 209)*

By every measure, "Composite Corporation" looks like a success. This service company located in the Midwest has enjoyed seven straight years of unparalleled, double-digit growth. Profits are good. Shareholders are pleased by the return they are getting on their investments. Demand for the company's services continues to grow, sometimes faster than the company can respond. Customer-satisfaction surveys, and the level of repeat business from customers, indicate a high level of satisfaction with the services provided by Composite. The company has recently received impressive recognition, including coverage in national newspapers, for the quality of its work.

During this same seven-year period, the organization's staff has more than doubled in size. For every opening there are many applicants, suggesting that Composite enjoys a reputation on the outside as a good place to work. The people hired have brought new levels of diversity and new energy to the company.

What's Wrong with This Picture?

From the outside looking in, nothing appears wrong. From inside looking out, the picture is quite different.

During its early years, Composite was a loosely structured company. New ideas and risk taking were encouraged, individuals enjoyed a lot of autonomy, irreverence was prized, and space was left in the workweek for celebrations. There was a belief, starting at the top, that the creativity evident in the organization was the result of being loosely structured. Too much control was feared more than a little chaos.

Along the way, about seven years ago, a new set of leaders were chosen to run Composite. These executives brought with them a different understanding and practice of leadership. They rightly observed that as Composite got larger, better systems and structures would be needed if the company were to be efficiently managed. So with the best of intentions the executives replaced a loosely structured process of governance with one that could easily be characterized as command-and-control: lots of policies, strict use of hierarchical structures, new bureaucratic systems, and most decisions made at the top. One employee remarked, "Maybe we needed some new systems and structures, but we've gone from the left ditch to the one on the right."

The change in the understanding and practice of leadership had varied impact on the staff. The first result was that employees lost their voice. People who used to poke and prod, and occasionally even tweak senior executives, became afraid to speak up. Irreverence stopped being seen as funny. Now employees were no longer involved in making decisions, especially the ones that mattered. Orders were given more than decisions were shared. Even though employees acknowledged that many of the decisions made by the new executives were good ones, the process by which they were made was disempowering and demeaning.

One example from Composite is telling. The president created a cross-organizational task force to consider an important change to the company's strategic direction. Members of the task force spent untold hours interviewing other employees, analyzing options, and developing a recommendation. Through a long and sometimes difficult process, the committee was able to reach consensus on the final recommendation. Because they were involved in the process, the task force members felt real ownership of the decision. They made their recommendation to the senior executives—and the executives decided, with no opportunity for further involvement by the task force to ignore the group's suggestion and move in an entirely different direction. Later it was learned that one executive had said all along that only one decision from the task force would be acceptable. The committee did its work without knowing this, and members learned only later that their decision was not the "right" one. The action by the senior executives took the "wind out of our sails," as one task force member said. It took the life and energy out of them. The story of the decision quickly spread through the organizational grapevine; as a result, others also became de-energized. It is a story still told in the organization whenever employees talk about top-down decisions that disenfranchise employees.

The people on the task force did not want Composite's executives to arbitrarily overrule a decision months in the making; they weren't used to that. If the initial recommendation was unacceptable, they wanted the executives to come back to the task force and engage in genuine conversation about why, and how to work together toward a shared decision.

Employees at Composite lost not only their voice but also their spirit. Though there seemed no pressing economic or business need to do so, the senior executives decided to eliminate several key positions, to "rightsize" the organization. It was necessary if the organization were to stay in "fighting shape," the executives argued, if it were to successfully "beat the competition" in the future. Eliminating positions ran counter to this organization's norms and practices, though; in the past employees, had agreed to share jobs rather than have a colleague laid off.

As have their counterparts in other organizations, after the downsizing the staff has begun working harder and longer to satisfy more and more customer demands. They've begun doing more with less. Before long, the stress is going to begin to take its toll. Those who stay will begin running on empty. There is no time for personal or professional renewal, no time to recharge batteries, to rekindle energy. Many of the brightest and most creative will choose not to stay. Turnover among professional staff is likely to snowball.

As employees lost their voice and spirit, creativity and innovation also waned. As the bureaucracy grew, and as command-and-control practices of leadership were exercised, individual employees started thinking and acting "inside the box." The organization became much less likely to invest in unproven projects, and individuals took fewer risks; instead, they did more of what they were told. Composite had built its reputation on offering services that were leading edge, but with the changes in the practice of leadership Composite began offering its customers adaptations of existing services more than new and innovative ones.

Yet another impact on the staff from the new understanding and practice of leadership was that Composite slowly moved from being a community to being an organization. Perhaps part of this was unavoidable; it could be argued that the increasing size and complexity alone made community less likely. But the executives contributed to the change by paying scant attention to important symbolic events. The use of rituals declined. Weekly and monthly celebrations gradually disappeared. Stories that once highlighted the fulfillment of the company's mission and values with particular clients were no longer told. Even the language changed. Such phrases as "take no prisoners," "stay lean and mean," and "kill the competition" entered the communications lexicon. Employees had once used the metaphor of family to describe the work community, but no more. Now Composite felt more like a typical bureaucratic organization. For the most part, customers were still served well, but the employees' spirits sagged, morale dropped, and cynicism grew. They were not as excited by, nor as committed to, their work.

A more subtle impact, and perhaps a more important one, is that the men and women of the organization came to feel that the company was losing sight of its mission and core values. Too many decisions were driven by short-term, bottom-line considerations, or so employees thought—even to the extent that service to customers suffered. Maybe it was not enough for customers to always notice, but employees did, and they didn't like it. Many employees had been attracted to Composite because of its congruence of deeply held personal values and personal sense of mission with the mission and values of the company, but now these values and the mission of Composite seemed to be shifting.

Now what do you make of this picture?

Here's a profitable, highly recognized company with more demand for its services that it can deliver. By most quantitative measures, it is still a success. But it is what one does not readily see and cannot easily measure that's important. Here is also a company with employees who give physical and mental energy to their work and by and large still deliver quality service, but who are not as enthused about it and no longer invest as much of themselves in it. Composite is losing its soul, and its staff is dispirited.

"Composite Corporation" is, of course, just what its name implies. It is a composite of actual organizations I have worked with in the past. The men and women of Composite are not unique, and their experience of life in their organization is different only in degree from what too many workers in too many organizations are experiencing—namely, that their work does not engage all their energies, does not provide them the sense of meaning and purpose for which they long, and does not call forth the best they have within them.

Two Threads

Two main threads weave through the story of Composite, and through the rest of this book. They are inextricably tied. They are leadership and spirit. This book hopes to offer new ways of understanding leadership and spirit, to show how leadership can liberate and elevate spirit and thus enliven people, and to demonstrate how spirit creates a vital and vibrant practice of leadership.

It may seem strange to you, as it has to me, to consider spirit as something connected to work. We are adept at compartmentalizing life. Work is just work (a way to earn a living, or so we say), and we think of spirit as something we attend to outside of work. Appropriately, we ask ourselves if work is really the right place to use spiritual energy. Leadership and spirit have more often been decoupled than coupled.

But spirit is a vital part of who we are. There are four domains that constitute our self: the physical, the mental, the emotional, and the spiritual. These four domains (in *Artful Work*, Dick Richards calls them energies) are interdependent. Our well-being requires that they interweave.

We know we use our mental energy at work. We use it to plan, organize, analyze, assess. We also move, sit, talk, play, laugh, travel, and work long hours, all of which require the use of our physical energy. We are aware that our emotions are also involved; at work, we feel anxious or safe, happy or sad, disappointed or delighted, included or left out—we allow our feelings of anger to inhibit us, while feelings of satisfaction and joy enable us. We recognize that work takes mental, physical, and emotional energy. But we are not so clear that it takes spiritual energy.

Once we realize that it is spirit that defines our self at the deepest levels of our being—that spirit enables us to offer our whole selves to the activity of leadership, to connect to others richly and rewardingly, and to give us deep sources of meaning—then we begin to understand its relationship to leadership and its importance in work. To the extent that we continue to turn attention away from matters of the spirit—that is, continue to believe that only physical, mental, and emotional energies are important at work—we go on ignoring a reality that could give new energy and vitality to us as individuals and our organizations.

The second thread in this tapestry is the thread of leadership. Clearly, we live in a time in which leadership is in vogue. All companies want it; individuals aspire to it. More books and articles have been written about it than any of us can read. And there are as many definitions of leadership as there are people who write about it.

Some of these definitions of leadership, when put into practice, leave no room for spirit, or worse, they wither it. There are practices of leadership that suck the life or vital energy—other names for spirit—out of people. To paraphrase the quote with which we started this chapter, this is the truth that must be named: organizations, and how we understand and practice leadership in them, are killing our spirit.

To be sure, how leadership is practiced is not the only force in organizations that is dispiriting. Jobs can be dispiriting. Jobs that do not engage our native gifts or fuel our talents drain energy from us. Burnout is the name we give to the end result of unrelenting job pressure. In *Working,* Studs Terkel quotes one professional he interviewed: "Jobs are not big enough for people. It isn't just the assembly-line worker whose job is too small for putting his spirit into it, you know? A job like mine, if you really put your spirit into it, you would sabotage it immediately. You don't dare. So you absent your spirit from it. My mind has been so divorced from my job, except as a source of income, it is really absurd" (1974, p. 521).

Like jobs, "-isms" are dispiriting. Racism, sexism, and ageism are always dispiriting, whether related to the practice of leadership or not. Stereotypes and prejudices always diminish the other person, always sap the energy of those discriminated against. But they also deplete the life of those who stereotype. Organizational structures often leave no room for spirit. Through the years, I have noticed that there seems to be a correlation between bureaucracy and the spirit of individuals. The greater the entrenched nature of the bureaucracy, the greater the lack of spirit within and among employees. We dispirit ourselves through the choices we make. We collude with those who exercise command and control by giving away our power and acting codependently. We complain about "them" and what they are doing to "us," but we don't choose to be authentic and honest when we have a chance to talk to them. We choose the safety and security of the status quo over work that would allow us to use our gifts and talents in life-giving, energy-producing ways.

It is far too easy to place all the blame for the lack of inspired performance in organizations on how leadership is practiced. The truth is more complex. But leadership *can* be dispiriting, and it doesn't have to be this way.

There is an understanding and practice of leadership that elevates spirit, honors the whole self, and encourages us to use all of our energies in the activities of leadership. There is an understanding and practice of leadership that taps into the best that is within us, that gives each of us an opportunity to be involved and engaged. There is an understanding and practice of leadership that helps us discover meaning in our work, that helps us live out our vision and make our mission manifest. It is an understanding that makes use of our spiritual energy, and it is understood as a spiritual experience. It leads to inspired performance.

When woven together, the two threads of leadership and spirit provide us with a new sense of hope. Hope that work can provide meaning and purpose. Hope that individuals can be their best and their whole self at work. Hope that we can create community out of workgroups and organizations. Hope that organizations can be profitable yet satisfying, competitive yet communal, productive yet life-giving.

An Analysis of Composite Corporation

With the threads of leadership and spirit in mind, let's analyze what's happening in Composite.

The employees of Composite Corporation, like the rest of us, bring specific hopes and expectations to their work. These aspirations come out of deeply felt human needs. Four of them stand out. The first, and maybe the most important, is this: *the employees want to be involved in the activity of leadership*.

The words *executive* and *leader* are often used interchangeably. The senior executives are the organization leaders, and leaders are the senior executives. Leadership is understood as the province of those in the executive suite, those with formal authority. In general, employees at Composite are not involved in leadership activities. Senior executives did not think that most employees wanted to take on leadership responsibilities or participate in leadership activities.

In Composite Corporation, leadership is still understood as an individual activity; the talk is about leaders more than about the activity of leadership. Leaders are "them"; leadership is something they do to us. But the men and women of Composite do not want this. They want to be involved in the process.

Seven years ago, the leaders at the top of Composite defined the mission of the organization, but the mission statement was not owned by the employees. It did not belong to them. It did not offer them a source of meaning. Putting the mission statement on plexiglass and hanging it conspicuously around the building did not make it meaningful. The leaders worked with an outside consultant to define a vision for the company—a vision they thought was daring and compelling—but the employees didn't buy. It wasn't theirs.

Even worse, top-down decisions on matters large and small, whether long-term strategies or day-to-day problems, deenergized the men and women of Composite. Not only were individuals not involved in making decisions but too often their voices were not heard at all before the decisions were made. There was no deep dialogue; information flowed from the top down. Efficiency and order were more important than involvement, control more important than collaboration, results more important than community. A command-and-control style, used constantly and over time, suffocates spirit.

The men and women of Composite also want to find meaning and purpose in what they do. Being engaged in work that is meaningful is a deeply felt human need. Each of us wants work that is imbued with purpose. Finding meaning and purpose is a spiritual act.

Early on, the employees talked of Composite as an organization that possessed spiritual anchors of just this kind. Work was a source of meaning and purpose; vision and values were shared. Because employees were in sync with the mission and values of the company, because of a shared sense that their work mattered and it was making a difference, working in the organization provided a deep sense of meaning. But no longer—or at least, not as much. Today, the shared sense of the employees is that the company has lost its moorings, that it is not as mission-oriented or values-driven, that the company is chasing the buck as much as it is doing work that matters. Many workers are disappointed and feel disconnected from the new Composite.

The third thing Composite employees want is to use all of their energies, to use their whole self, in their work. The needs of organizations have changed; the expectations of workers have also changed. We now look to the work we do to provide a source of meaning and purpose that we used to seek only in the church or synagogue, the family, or the community. For many workers today, the workplace is the new neighborhood, the place where they find community if they are to find it at all. We are no longer content to compartmentalize ourselves. We are no longer willing to be "empty raincoats, nameless numbers on a payroll, role occupants, the raw material of economics or sociology." At one time we used all of our energies in our work. Farmers and self-employed craftsmen, to name but two examples, invested their whole selves—their physical, mental, emotional, and spiritual energy—in their work. For many of them, there was no separation between life and work.

But then expectations began to change. With the dawning of the industrial age, organizations came to think they needed only the physical energy of their employees. Muscle and brawn mattered, not mind, heart, or spirit. Frederick Winslow Taylor, the father of scientific management, was known for his ability to precisely calculate how much physical energy organizations could and should expect from each worker each day. Taylor argued that workers were not paid to think—and that in fact it would be dangerous for them to do so. Workers, Taylor said, should ask only two questions: "For whom do I work?" and "What does he want me to do right now?" Workers were expected to compartmentalize themselves: take their physical selves to work, but leave mental, emotional, and spiritual energy at home, or at least locked securely in the trunk of the car out in the company parking lot.

At the start of the information age, expectations changed again. Now organizations needed individuals to bring enormous mental capacity to work, and to use their mental energy to create and produce. The knowledge worker became an important asset—in some companies, the most important asset. Individuals still had to use physical energy, but now the use of mental energy was also required.

Organizations, and the executives who ran them, began to slowly realize, and at least give tacit acknowledgment to, the importance of emotional energy. We learned that *emotion* and *motivation* come from the same root word; that it is the way we feel about the work we do, not the work itself, that is motivating or demotivating. To get the motivation and commitment needed, at least some executives learned to hear and pay attention to the feelings of individual workers. A lot of what we have learned through the years about how to motivate employees (such as the power and importance of positive recognition) spoke to the growing awareness of the importance of emotional energy.

Today, the needs of organizations and the expectations of workers have changed yet again. In the fast-paced, white-water world in which organizations now operate, those that are to succeed need employees who offer the best they have within them. The work of organizations must now be done with creativity and passion, with commitment and dedication. Doing this requires that we use all of our energies: mental, physical, emotional, and spiritual. Organizations need for us to offer our best selves, and we want to and we will—if the situation warrants it, if practices of leadership invite it.

In the early part of its history, Composite Corporation had practices of leadership that engaged all the energies of its people. Work was inspiring. It tapped into the best that employees had within them, and it required that they go beyond the logical and rational to truths coming from their depths. It called for full use of their gifts and talents; it asked that they be creative and imaginative. Today, work in Composite Corporation requires the use of physical and mental energy, and sometimes emotional energy, but it does not ask for people to use their spiritual energy.

Consciously or unconsciously, the executives of Composite Corporation developed systems, structures, and leadership practices that squeezed the spirit out of the men and women of the company (or at least sent it underground). From one perspective, the mistake of the executives was a mistake of omission: there simply was no consideration of the role and importance of spirit in the work of the organization. There was no sense that spiritual energy was important, nor expectation that it was to be used. This inattention to the fact that spirit matters was evident in how the executives handled the spiritual dis-ease employees felt after the downsizing.

David Noer, a friend and former colleague, has written eloquently about layoff-survivor sickness, the emotional dis-ease that is experienced by those who stay on after downsizing. "It begins," he writes, "with a deep sense of violation. It ends with angry, sad, depressed employees, consumed in their attempt to hold onto jobs that have become devoid of joy, spontaneity, and personal relevancy, and with the organization attempting to survive in a competitive, global environment with a risk-averse, depressed work force. This is no way to lead a life, and no way to run an organization" (1993, p. 3). This vivid description fits many of the staff who remained at Composite after downsized employees left.

Compounding the problem for those suffering from layoff-survivor sickness is the fact that the executives at Composite refused to acknowledge that the sickness was real. Instead, they operated on the assumption that those who stayed would be glad to have their jobs, would be ready to continue business as usual, would even be ready to take on extra work to keep the business moving forward. As in most organizations that have downsized, what we have in Composite are dispirited workers and massive denial by their leaders that this is the case. Obviously, layoff-survivor sickness cannot be cured, and the wounds cannot be healed, so long as executives expect even more physical and mental exertion from the wounded survivors but pay scant attention to their emotional health and their spirit. At its core, layoff-survivor sickness is a problem of spirit, and it must be dealt with as such.

But from another angle, the mistake of the executives was what they did: they put systems (policies, procedures, processes) in place that were adhered to so tightly that there was no room for spontaneity or spirit. They created organizational structures that made rational sense but had the unintentional consequence of creating more competition and less collaboration, more control and less community. They used an understanding and practice of leadership that caused spirit to wither and wane.

There is yet a fourth need individuals have that was not being met for the employees of Composite. *Like each of us, they have a need to be seen as individuals, and they want to be involved in community.* There are a yin and a yang to this for the people of Composite, just as there are for all of us. We are unique individuals who prize our autonomy, and we want to be part of community.

Part of our development is to grow in our awareness of self and to recognize our uniqueness, foster a sense of independence, and begin to accept responsibility for ourselves. Psychologically, this process is known as individuation; it means becoming more fully ourselves, each of us becoming our true and whole self. Because spirit is part of who we are, individuation also includes broadening and deepening our awareness of the spirit that breathes life into us, animates us, and connects us. If we do not complete this process, we too easily lose our sense of ourselves. We let others define us. Our self-esteem is dependent on the approval of others. We accommodate too quickly to the needs of others. We go along to get along.

There is a difference, though, between individuation and rugged individualism. We often confuse the two. We believe that completing the process of individuation means that we must always stand on our own two feet, make tough decisions by ourselves, always be independent. We think that being strong means being heroic, and conversely that any sign of dependence is a weakness. Being part of community and acting interdependently is seen as being too soft, especially in a business community like Composite. We fear that we cannot be ourselves and yet be part of community. Paradoxically, though, we understand ourselves, and even find ourselves, in the context of community.

Linking the individual and the community is more than just a human need; it is often an organizational imperative. Phil Jackson, until recently the coach of basketball's Chicago Bulls, put it this way: "More than anything I wanted to build a team that would blend individual talent with heightened group consciousness. . . . Creating a successful team—whether it is an NBA champion or a record-setting sales force—is essentially a spiritual act. It requires individuals involved to surrender their self-interest for the greater good so that the whole adds up to more than the sum of the parts" (1995, p. 5).

Instead of doing this, the leaders at Composite confused individuation with rugged individualism. They understood leadership as individual, heroic effort. They adopted for their own a slogan Ross Perot used in the last presidential campaign: "Eagles don't flock." They made the critical decisions themselves, often without any consultation with those who would be affected. They used hierarchy to communicate information and to maintain control.

Individual effort was recognized and rewarded. Use of the language of "family" and community ceased.

Composite Is Not Unique

What is happening in Composite Corporation is happening to other organizations, and to individuals in them, across this country. Not exactly the same situation, but a similar dynamic, a practice of leadership that unintentionally withers the spirit of the people. The picture looks much the same, and it is not pretty. Across the board, today's workers are by and large a dispirited lot.

To make sure the point is clear, let me reiterate. Being dispirited is different from experiencing such uncomfortable emotions as frustration or anger or disappointment. There are times when we feel hurt or angry and yet deeply alive, full of energy. At times, unpleasant emotions inspire us. By contrast, being dispirited is the experience of having the wind knocked completely out of us, of having no sense of vitality or energy for the work we do, of feeling lifeless. It is being "used up" (and today, "42 percent of all Americans leave work at the end of each day feeling used up"; Handy, 1998, p. 17). The experience is intense.

You can hear the sound of dispirited people as you listen to the stories they tell. Stories of bosses who throw things in meetings, or storm out of them in a huff. Stories of long-term employees being fired and given only a few minutes to clean out their desks—and that with an escort. Stories of individuals feeling they've been cut off at the knees in public, of executives holding staff up to public ridicule. Stories of organizational leaders who manage by mood: charming one moment, demeaning the next. Stories of executives who "take no prisoners," who insist that it is "my way or the highway." Stories of leaders who micromanage, who turn things over but never turn them loose. These are stories that illustrate how leaders can suck vital energy and spirit out of people.

Other stories are more subtle, but the impact is just as real. Stories of individuals being left out of important decisions, decisions that affect them profoundly. Stories of individuals who are "promoted" into less meaningful work, work that does not make good use of their talents and energies. Stories of executives who create unnecessary competition among people in the same group or department because "it motivates the troops." Stories of executives who may deserve respect but who expect deference.

So here's the picture: today we have thousands of individuals who give physical and mental energy to their work but don't invest their souls and spirit in it. Work is not worth that.

Pollster Daniel Yankelovich noticed this trend years ago. "The leaders who run organizations," he said, "do not really understand today's work force: tens of millions of well-educated Americans, proud of their achievements, zealous of their freedom, motivated by new values, with substantial control over production, and ready to raise their production if given proper encouragement" (Galagan, 1988, p. 37).

The picture is clear: we are a dispirited workforce, a workforce that gives our heads and hands, but not our heart and spirit, to our jobs. And we have organizational leaders who, at best, are not aware that this is true and, at worst, add to the problem by how they manage and lead.

The concepts of leadership and spirit come with a lot of baggage, but they are too important for us to relinquish them. We need to repack the bags, leaving behind some of the old definitions and concepts that do not serve us well, and packing in their place new understandings of leadership and spirit that allow us to engage all the energies of the members of the work community.

Leadership, Spirit, and the Bottom Line

"But," the hard-headed realist asks, "can we be concerned about issues of spirit and still be as profitable? Isn't the purpose of business business? Is business the right place to look for meaning and fulfillment? Don't executives need to keep their eye on return to share-holders rather than on helping individuals to find a sense of pur-pose in their work?"

Empirically, I know of no hard evidence suggesting that com-panies that weave together spirit and leadership are more prof-itable. (I also know that we need to be careful of empirical data. Businesses on the list of "excellent" companies one year are often in the doldrums the next.) There is anecdotal data, though, sug-gesting that companies having begun the process of weaving spirit and leadership are doing well by doing good. The stories of some of those companies are told in the chapters that follow.

The reverse is clearly not true. Focusing only on the bottom line does not work—not even to enhance the bottom line. The authors of *Built to Last*, James C. Collins and Jerry Porras, report that, contrary to current dogma, one of the successful habits of companies enduring over time is that they have been driven more by core ideology than by profit goals. "Contrary to business school doctrine," they write, "we did not find 'maximizing shareholder wealth' or 'profit maximization' as the dominant driving force or primary objective through the history of most visionary companies" (1994, p. 55).

We tend to think that focusing on spirit and maintaining prof-itability are opposites, that we can focus on either one or the other. One of the important challenges facing us as we come to the end of this century is to learn how to be "both-and" people: to be hard-headed realists while paying attention to spirit. To keep a focus on the bottom line while making meaning in our work communities. We can be nimble and flexible enough to do both. In later chap-ters, there are examples of women and men learning to be both-and people. This is a both-and book.

But let's be honest. A central thesis of this book is that organi-zations have to be focused on more than improving the bottom line, as important as that is. Improving value to shareholders is not the kind of mission that energizes and enthuses people. We can improve the return to shareholders and *still* be a miserable, dispirited people.

If organizations are ever going to make full and good use of the energies of their people, if individuals are ever going to give the best they have within themselves in service to the organization, then work and the organization must leave room for spirit. It is only when we do this that the work we do in organizations, where we spend so much of our time, is worth the investment of our lives.

Chapter Two

Understanding and Experiencing Spirit

It is the spirit that motivates, that calls upon a
man's reserves of dedication and effort, that decides
whether he will give his best or
just enough to get by.

—*Peter Drucker (1954, p. 144)*

Spirit is a word used a lot in our everyday experience. Coaches want good team spirit; military leaders want esprit de corps; managers want inspired performance. Some even drink spirits. But it is only in recent years that we have begun to think about leadership and spirit. For some, the link between leadership and spirit is clear; for others it is not; and for still others the thought of a link is unsettling, even disturbing. As a friend says, it sounds too much like "praying for profits."

Over the past several years, as I have talked about the link between leadership and spirit in countless conversations with businesspeople from all walks of life, and in many different settings, I have heard all sorts of questions:

"But what is spirit? How do you define it?"

"Is spirit real?"

"How can I know if I'm experiencing spirit?"

"Don't we need to be careful about introducing a religious concept into work?"

"Are there really businesses in which spirit is discussed and talked about?"

These questions reflect curiosity, and uneasiness, about spirit. We want to connect the various dimensions of our life but are not sure that we can, or even that we ought to. We don't like the disconnect between the way we see ourselves as persons and as workers, but we are not sure there is anything we can do about it. The questions also reflect underlying assumptions about spirit, about what it is and where it operates—and the where is not always the workplace. Even those who would like leadership and spirit to be linked are not sure the two can be in fast-paced, rapidly changing, technologically oriented, bottom-line-focused organizations, and in a world where scientism and rationalism still rule.

This chapter tries to answer these questions, and others like them, showing that spirit is something we experience in ordinary events, and that it exists to some extent within us and between us. It is time to rethink spirit, to understand that it is part of our everyday experiences, and to weave together leadership and spirit.

I hope in this chapter and throughout this book to make spirit more understandable, to create awareness of how we can and do connect to it in everyday experiences of leadership and life. But I do not want to take all the mystery out of it. Instead, I invite you to look at spirit through another set of eyes, what Ken Wilber (1998) calls the "eyes of contemplation." We spend so much of our lives, and especially our lives at work, looking at things though the "eyes of the flesh" (empirically) or through the "eyes of the mind" (rationally) that we sometimes believe what we see through these sets of eyes is all that exists. If this seems true for you, then it may appear strange, if not impossible, to see through eyes of contemplation. If so, I ask you to suspend judgment, at least temporarily. I invite you to move beyond empiricism and rationalism and connect (or perhaps reconnect) to spirit.

What Is Spirit?

Spirit comes from the Latin word *spiritus*, which means breath, as in the breath of life. Spirit is the unseen force that breathes life into us, enlivens us, gives energy to us. Spirit is the "other"—

the life force—that weaves through and permeates all of our experiences.

Spirit works within us. It helps define the true, real, unique self that is us. It confirms our individuality. It works within us to nudge us toward what Thomas Merton called our "hidden wholeness." We are who we are because of spirit.

Spirit also works between and among us. It connects us to everything that exists. It is because of the work of spirit that we experience deep communion with others, experience ourselves as part of something much larger, experience connectedness to all of life.

Several years ago, George Leonard, former senior editor at *Look* magazine, expressed much the same idea. What I have called spirit he called the silent pulse. The ideas are similar if not identical. Leonard said, "To be human, it seems clear, is to have a personal identity. This identity is unique. . . . It survives death. Each of us has our own inner pulse . . . it finds expression in the way we walk, talk, sing, write, shake hands, make love. The inner pulse is stable and consistent at the most fundamental level" (1978, pp. 55, 62). But the silent pulse does more than extend to us our identity. In Leonard's words, "we are completely, firmly, absolutely connected with all of existence" (p. 87). This, too, is the work of the silent pulse.

Spirit is always present, and it is everywhere present. Whoever you are, wherever you are, whatever you are doing in this moment, spirit is present. It may be outside your conscious awareness, but it is present. It is present in the places we work and in our leadership activities, whether we notice it or not. It is not something that has to be developed or formed. It needs to be *uncovered*, not discovered. Uncovering spirit does not require that we develop a new set of skills or abilities so much as learn to reconnect to it. It is part of each of us, not just the special few we call mystics. We each experience it, at least sometimes, in our life and our work.

Just as we can mask our feelings or deny our behavior, so too we can suppress spirit. We can cover it up. Our busyness, our need to please others, our quest for status and our yearning for approval, our attempts to maintain a front can all cover and constrain spirit. But spirit is still there, still part of who we are, still working within us and among us. Our need is to be in touch with spirit, to acknowledge its importance, and to engage in behaviors—including leadership behaviors—that liberate and elevate it.

Spirit and Religion

Talk of spirit often conjures up images of religious belief systems. Because of this, I hasten to add that when I talk of spirit, in this book and elsewhere, I am not talking about religion, and I am not proposing that we introduce religion into our world of work. I do not believe that one has to be religious to be spiritual, or vice versa.

When I use the word *spirit*, I am not talking about being religious or about accepting and following the beliefs of a particular religion. I am not even talking about spirit as always achieving an elevated state of mind or being through prayer or meditation—as important as these may be, and as sometimes happens when we experience spirit in the ordinary events of life and work. For me, being spiritual is about *being fully human*, about integrating all the energies that are part of us. It is about connecting to that life force that defines us and connects us.

Spirit and spirituality are better understood as phenomena that are prior to and different from any particular expression of religion. To be sure, religion can be a pathway to spirit and a nurturer of it; the one can and sometimes does complement the other. But religion, and particular practices of it, can be a barrier to the experience of spirit. My personal experience is that dogma held too tightly can inhibit the experience of spirit. It is important to the tapestry we are weaving that we learn to talk about spirit separately from any particular religious belief system.

Years ago, Abraham Maslow stated the case this way: "I want to demonstrate that spiritual values have a naturalistic meaning, that they are not the exclusive possession of organized churches, that they do not need supernatural concepts to validate them, that they are well within the jurisdiction of a suitably enlarged science, and that, therefore, they are the general responsibility of all mankind" (1970, p. 33). Maslow saw spirituality as a human phenomenon, one more basic than any particular expression of religion. This is the key point: *spirit is as natural as anything else in the natural world.* Understood in this way, spirit is an essential part of each of us. This is the understanding of spirit that I use in this book.

Is Spirit Real?

In a scientific age, believing in an unseen force that enlivens and animates, that weaves through and saturates all experience, is pushing the envelope too far for some people. Not all of us understand it as a natural phenomenon. Peter Vaill recently wrote that "spirituality is an aspect of our experience that is truly undiscussible in objectivist science" (1998, p. 28). For the rationalists and empiricists among us, believing in the reality of spirit can be a bit much.

It has been a bit much for me for much of my life. By personality preference, I consider something real and true if it is known to one of my senses—if I can touch it, see it, hear it, taste it, smell it, then it is real. I like to make decisions based on logical, rational consideration of data, not on intuition or hunch or gut feel. I am more of a realist than an idealist, understanding myself as doing better with hard and cold facts (the language of such expressions is interesting, isn't it?) rather than imaginative ideas. Even in the religious tradition that provided my early grounding, the United Methodist Church, I did not experience much emphasis on the everyday working of spirit. From my early days on, religion emphasized a belief system (the use of mental energy) more than it did inner experience.

At the same time, as I struggled to be open to diverse experiences, I realized that some of the most important and most defining realities are those not experienced through my senses: a sure and clear connectedness in a one-to-one relationship, awareness that something special and different is happening in a group of which I am a part, feeling at one with the universe as I appreciate the sun rising on a new day while in the mountains, even the synchronistic moment of thinking of a friend and then he calls.

For too long, I lived with the mistaken belief that only those things that are tangible are real. Perhaps you have, also. It is part of our scientific, rational mind-set. We think that for something to be real it must be physical and material, known to one of the five senses, empirically provable. This is an illusion that does not serve us well; because of it we discount the importance of spirit. What I have come to comprehend is that my senses help me know the material, but I have to go beyond my senses to know spirit. Although spirit takes me beyond my five senses, it can still be understood and experienced as natural, like everything else in the natural world. Spirit is nonmaterial, but it is real. Today, bridging the visible and invisible, seeing as real the tangible *and* the intangible, and experiencing the unseen force called spirit in all aspects of my life is one of my core purposes. I now believe we can understand spirit, experience it, and engage in practices of leadership that acknowledge and honor it.

The Experience of Spirit

We also typically connect spirit only to the extraordinary experiences of life, to holy or transcendent events. We think we only experience spirit in church or synagogue, in meditation or prayer, in solitary walks in nature. We use life in monasteries and convents as a symbol of how men and women connect to spirit. Spirit does weave through those experiences, but it also saturates the ordinary experiences of work and life. We experience spirit in the midst of our busy and active lives as well as in moments of solitude. The seeds of spirit are planted, are nurtured, and grow in ordinary experiences in the midst of our everyday lives, and this is where we must reconnect to it. Martin Buber, the famous Jewish theologian, called this the "hallowing of the everyday"—the determination to find spirit in the ongoing and ordinary experiences of life.

Several years ago, Sue Bender wrote about finding spirit in the ordinary in her exquisite book *Plain and Simple*. A harried urban Californian, Bender felt her life was, by her own definition, "like a crazy quilt, a pattern I hated. Hundreds of scattered, unrelated, stimulating fragments, each going off in its own direction, creating lots of frantic energy. There was no overall structure to hold the pieces together. The Crazy Quilt was a perfect metaphor for my life" (1989, p. 4). She was called to live with the Amish by the enchantment she had with their quilts, and by her love of the faceless dolls made by them. What she learned was that every activity of the Amish—from cooking to washing dishes, from planting tomatoes to canning them—was a spiritual act. The Amish did not hurry through one activity to get to another. No activity, no matter how mundane it might appear to others, was a burden to them. The Amish experienced spirit in the most ordinary activities of life.

For the past several years, two colleagues and I have hosted a Spirit and Leadership Conference at the start of each new year. Participants have joined us from across the United States, and from several other countries, to cocreate an event in which we could share our understandings of spirit and reflect on the link of leadership and spirit. To help get ready for the conference participants commit to do some reflecting and writing ahead of time on how spirit is experienced in their personal and professional lives. The answers vary a great deal, but one theme that emerges from many of the responses is the connection of spirit to the everyday occurrences of life:

> Experiencing spirit comes down to the power of ordinary experiences . . . for me it is best reflected in relationships, whether they be professional or personal.

> The experience is all around me when I look for it . . . it happened recently in our leadership team when everyone expressed their personal goals and then related them to our overall team goals. We agreed to be part of something larger than ourselves.

I experience spirit in small and sometimes unobtrusive ways. For instance, I think of moments when obfuscation for the purpose of manipulating outcomes was magnificently overridden by honesty and integrity. Or when the true needs of a person were attended to rather than the projected needs. Or when people were supported for reasons of truly contributing to their development, rather than for the purposes of making the developer look good.

For me, personally, I have realized that I experience spirit when I am being myself. That is, being kind to people, respecting their perspectives, giving voice to the truth as I know it, finding ways to experience joy in work.

Spirit breathes life into us in all of these everyday experiences. It is a natural occurrence. It adds new vitality and new energy to moments and activities that otherwise might be mundane.

To be sure, we also encounter spirit in events that appear extraordinary. One example is known as synchronicity. Synchronicity is an experience of the link between what goes on in our inner psyche and some external event, between our inner and outer worlds. Carl Jung described three types of synchronicity:

1. A link between an internal thought (I think of you . . .) and an external happening (. . . and you call)

2. A dream or mental image that matches an event happening at some other place

3. A sixth sense or a dream that something will happen in the future and, in fact, it does

Joseph Jaworski has written simply and eloquently about how synchronicity is experienced in the practice of leadership. In *Synchronicity: The Inner Path of Leadership* (1996), he tells a personal story about the third type of synchronicity. Jaworski spent four years on assignment with Royal Dutch Shell's worldwide scenario-planning team, a move that had been forecast by his wife, Mavis. Some five years before starting the assignment, Jaworski was in London with Mavis on the steps of St. Paul's cathedral when she said, "Joseph, I want you to know something I am certain of. In the next few years, you will move back to London with the family and me. You will do important work for a very large multinational company" (1996, p. 142).

Jung described these experiences as meaningful coincidences. He suggested that the link between them could not be understood by typical views of cause and effect. We cannot understand the link by using only our mental energy. Instead, Jung believed that for synchronicity to happen, the space between one person and another, between the internal and external events, could not be empty. The space, he said, was filled by the "collective unconscious." This is, from my perspective, another name for spirit, the unseen force that weaves through and permeates all of our experiences.

I hesitate to mention synchronistic experiences of spirit because I fear it might detract from the central point: that spirit is known to each of us in everyday and ordinary life. I include it because synchronicity, like other experiences of spirit, is available to all of us. But we don't usually think of these events in this way. We dismiss them as kooky or just too new age. When a synchronistic event happens to us we think of it as mere coincidence, or, as a friend said to me, "purely a matter of mathematics." But spirit, no matter how faint or disguised, continues to stir within each of us and among us, and experiences we dismiss as mere coincidence offer us a new view of reality.

Manifestations of Spirit

There are many ways that spirit manifests itself to us, many ways we can know of its presence, from the ordinary to the extraordinary events of life. Spirit manifests itself not only in events but also within us, between and among us, and in communities.

Spirit Works Within Us

One of my first realizations of the link of leadership and spirit was when I saw that at various times in my work I felt much more alive and complete. There are times when my role in leadership activities calls on me to use my gifts, and at those times I feel more enthusiasm, more excitement, more animation. There are times in leadership roles when the work being done is congruent with my personal sense of mission and values, and I sense renewal and wholeness and power. There are times at work when I know I am being myself. At these times, I feel inspired. There are also times, of course, when my work in leadership processes is important but not meaningful, when it takes more energy than it gives, and when I leave at the end of the day more frustrated by things left undone than satisfied by the things accomplished. We cannot expect to feel renewed and reenergized every day, but we can find the right kind of work, and we can involve ourselves in leadership activities such that we come closer to experiencing the guiding energy of spirit at work. Deep inside, we can experience the breath of life that is spirit.

Partly because of my reflection on the times when I feel alive at work, I have asked people in many groups to tell me when they too feel most alive at work. The assumption behind my question is that when we feel most alive and find new sources of vitality and energy, we are experiencing spirit. I've heard many answers:

"When I am being the best I can be."

"When I wake up in the middle of the night with a fresh idea on how I can solve a nagging problem."

"When I am authentic and speak the truth, even if I know that what I say won't be popular."

"When I know that I am fully using the talents I have, and using them in work that is important."

"When I am in a lot of pain—really hurting—but at the same time feel alive and in touch."

"When I meditate or write in my journal and develop new perspectives on the work I am doing."

"When I have acted on my core values in various leadership situations."

In one way, the answers are similar. All these people experience spirit internally, within themselves. Too often, we tend to believe that the things that matter are external to us. We attempt to explain what happens in our personal and professional lives as caused by forces external to self. We think and act as though the source of happiness is out there: a house, a car, the right mate, a better job. We even think that spirit is out there, in a church or synagogue, or in nature. Spirit is "out there"; but we can also experience it "in here," deep within the core of our being. We experience spirit intrapersonally.

In another way, these people's answers reflect a difference. Some feel most alive and in the presence of spirit when engaged in a solitary activity: journaling, reflecting, running. Others experience spirit within themselves in the midst of an activity: being creative, solving a problem, helping a colleague. Both are important. There is a tendency to think that spirit and spirituality are connected to solitary activities, disciplines such as prayer and meditation. Sometimes they are. But at other times, spirit is experienced in the midst of an involved and active life.

Roy is one of the deepest thinkers and most outstanding leaders I have known. He consistently acts on his core values and maintains his integrity, even if there is a cost (financial or otherwise) in doing so. He treats his direct reports with deep respect, honoring them as individuals who have diverse gifts and perspectives. He gets results.

Roy is also intentional about staying in touch with his spirit, with spending time, as he says, in "that room of my house." After lengthy meetings, you can find him taking a leisurely walk by himself, clearing his head and finding his center. Once after a three-day offsite meeting at a mountain retreat, while others were preparing to return home, Roy left for time alone in the mountains. He connects with spirit in solitude.

As I suggested earlier, this is not how I experience spirit. I experience it interpersonally amid a busy life: when I find congruence between my gifts and my work, and when in leadership roles I act on my deepest values. Parker Palmer has written an eloquent book, *The Active Life*, in which he suggests that he also finds spirit in activity and with others: "Contemporary images of what it means to be spiritual tend to value the inward search over the outward act, silence over sound, solitude over interaction, centeredness and quietude and balance over engagement and animation and struggle" (1990, p. 2).

Whether in solitude or in the midst of an active life, each of us can (and on occasion we do) experience spirit working within us, breathing new energy and new vitality into us.

We Experience Spirit Interpersonally

We connect to the unseen force we call spirit in our relationships. We experience spirit at those times we feel connected (or if you will, when we feel a sense of deep communion) with another person.

In *I and Thou* (1970, published posthumously), Buber described one way this happens. We often use another person as an "it," as the means to an end. The other person is used instrumentally. We want or need something from the other, and we work the relationship so that we get it. All of us—organizational executives, managers, and workers alike—are guilty of this. Whenever someone is treated as an object, as just another box on the organizational chart, he or she is being treated as an it. When employees are seen as assets (the language is revealing: "a human resource"), valuable only to the extent that they increase shareholder value, those employees are being treated as an it. Employees used as pawns in political games of one-upmanship are being used instrumentally. One worker using another for selfish gain is treating the other as an it. An individual talked *about* rather than *to* becomes an object or an it. Not just in work situations are individuals treated as an it. The same thing happens between best friends, between lovers, between parent and child, between husband and wife. In all of these relationship, one person can use another to get what is wanted. "I-it" relationships are always dispiriting.

Buber suggested another option: relating to the other as a "thou," relating out of deep respect and honoring who the other is as an individual. In an I-thou relationship the other is not treated as the means to an end, but rather as the end. When we connect with and honor the person who lives inside the other, we are experiencing the person as a thou. I-thou relationships have a special vitality. We are different, our sense of connectedness changes, we see the other differently. Just as I-it relationships happen both at work and outside, so do those that are I-thou.

I-thou relationships are similar to (if not the same as) what Max De Pree, former president of the well-known and highly respected furniture manufacturer Herman S. Miller, called *covenantal relationships*:

> Broadly speaking, there are two types of relationships in industry. The first and most easily understood is the contractual relationship. The contractual relationship covers the quid pro quo of working together. . . . But more is needed, particularly today when the majority of workers are, essentially, volunteers . . . a legal contract almost invariably breaks down under the inevitable duress of conflict and change . . . a contract has nothing to do with reaching our potential. . . . Covenantal relationships, on the other hand, induce freedom, not fear. Covenantal relationships rest on shared commitment to ideas, to issues, to values, to goals, and to management processes. Words such as love, warmth, personal chemistry are certainly pertinent . . . they fill deep needs and enable us to have meaning and to be fulfilling. Covenantal relationships reflect unity and grace and poise. They are an expression of the sacred nature of relationships [1989, p. 51].

Several years ago, I was working with some senior-level executives of a major division of a multinational company. The president was a fast-charging, high-potential executive in his late thirties. He was a no-nonsense, hard-nosed boss. The other executives were all bright and aggressive. But relationships weren't cooperative, and they weren't functioning well as a team. The vice presidents tended to fear the president, and with each other they were more competitive than collaborative. I was trying to help them assess their strengths and weaknesses as a team.

As part of the assessment process, the seven executives on the team participated in a simulation, one that replicated the challenges they faced in their organization. During the simulations and the debriefings that followed, it became very apparent that one of the vice presidents was being scapegoated. He was blamed for the poor decisions that were made, for the opportunities that were missed, for the strategic wrong turns that were taken. Even the president joined in the finger-pointing and blaming. Among other things, during the debriefings we talked about this scapegoating and its negative impact on team functioning.

On the evening of the second day, I was sitting outside with the president and the vice president who had been scapegoated. It was a beautiful and inviting setting, one in which it was easy to relax and talk. With no prodding from me, the president brought up the scapegoating that had happened, acknowledged his culpability, even expressed his concern that had he created relationships in which the victimized vice president and others were afraid of him. The president was honest and open, even vulnerable. The vice president was initially taken aback. He didn't know quite how to respond, but somewhat hesitantly he began to talk about his fear of the president and his anger toward colleagues who had done in the simulation what they did in real life: blame him when things went wrong.

This brief conversation—this I-thou moment—did not solve the problems that existed between the president and vice president or among team members, but they did hear each other and affirm each other. It was a moment in time in which the president and vice president later reported that they felt a deep sense of vitality and energy, that their relationship had received a breath of new life. Leadership and spirit were linked. The moment gave them a reference point that would prove useful for them in the future.

We Experience Spirit in Community

We also experience spirit—a breath of life—in community. Most often, teams and workgroups are just that: individuals come together as a group for ongoing work or for special short-term task force assignments, and they stay centered on accomplishing their work as efficiently and effectively as possible. They use mental and physical energy, but not spiritual energy, to get their work done. Teams, workgroups, and task forces can accomplish their purpose and do good work well without becoming community, without experiencing or using spiritual energy.

But occasionally a team becomes community. A breakthrough happens; team members find a new source of energy, honor others as they are being honored, and find new meaning in the shared undertaking. Not long ago, I watched this happen in a cross-functional management team at work. It was a team formed some two years earlier in the merger of two large companies. They were at loggerheads. Try as they might, they could not agree on future strategic direction. One faction wanted to stay the course with their present strategy. It had worked for years; it made sense; they were comfortable with it. They operated with an "if it ain't broke, don't fix it" mind-set. The other faction, which included most employees from the company being acquired, were ready to try a different strategy, one that had worked for them previously. They argued, in effect, that "it's when it ain't broke that you ought to fix it." The two perspectives both had some validity, but in conversations this interpretation was not acknowledged. People talked past each other, defended their own positions more than working to understand another perspective, and either denied or tried to fix conflicts as quickly as they surfaced. They were stymied.

Just at it looked as though the group would fragment, one team member stopped the constant back-and-forth long enough to ask about the assumptions underlying the opposite perspective. Then he listened, really listened, to the response. Slowly, a new sort of conversation began, and with it new levels of understanding arose, including open acknowledgment of the real differences that divided them. One team member whispered to me, "Something different is happening here." In the ensuing conversation, they became more honest and less defensive, more open to what the other was saying. They found commonalities and a sense of connectedness amid difference. They moved from narrow self-interest to heightened interest in the needs of the whole work community. They found ways to maintain integrity while searching for common ground. They experienced a breath of new life. That unseen force we call spirit weaves in and through groups and helps them move toward community.

I have observed other groups become community as they work on important activities that provide an overarching sense of meaning and purpose, for instance in creating a vision for the organization, articulating mission (the *why* of the work), or clarifying core values. Annual goals and objectives, and the budgets related to them, tend to be logical and rational; preparing them usually only requires mental and physical energy. Goals and objectives are important, but they are seldom compelling. A statement of vision is different. When done well, it comes from the depths, from the stirrings beneath the surface of logic and emotion, down where things matter most deeply. Creating and articulating a shared vision is essentially a spiritual activity that helps a workgroup move toward community.

We can even encounter spirit in special-occasion communities. Earlier, I mentioned the working session on spirit and leadership that two colleagues have joined me in hosting for several years. Most of the individuals who accept our invitation to cocreate the experience with us by and large do not known each other before the sessions start. We are a group of strangers drawn together by common interest, commitment to reflect and to share, and willingness to be open to the unseen force called spirit. We use the technology of open space, designed by Harrison Owen, as the way of structuring and creating our experience. Open space invites all participants to engage in the activity of leadership; anyone can convene a session on an issue of personal importance. The technology of open space elicits spirit and fosters community. Community is also fostered in these conferences by the personal stories that are shared, by the deep dialogue that occurs, and by the various art forms—movement, music, poetry—that are used.

We Experience Spirit in Companies

Spirit can be experienced in communities as large as an entire company. It may not happen often, but it does happen. TDIndustries is one such company. This Texas-based company is a mechanical contracting and service company that works in the competitive world of commercial and residential construction. It is no place for the weak of heart or for the practice of soft leadership. It is the kind of company where you would reasonably expect to find a macho culture, command-and-control leadership, concern for profits more than people. Not the kind of organization where you would expect to hear expressions of love, see employees being treated as family, or listen to talk of spirit.

But spirit is acknowledged, engaged, and talked about at TDI. In fact, the opening line of the film made to celebrate the company's first fifty years is, "If one word summarizes the first remarkable years of TDI, it is spirit."

Leadership and spirit is linked at TDIndustries through very specific practices. In 1952, Jack Lowe Sr., the founder of the company, decided to ask employees to become partners through stock ownership rather than put the company in debt. The employees said yes. The author of a 1987 history of the company, Ashley Cheshire, said of this decision that "it established the fact that Jack believed his employees were more than hired help; they were people who deserved a chance at the long-range benefits of the work they were doing. Jack wanted the company to be a place where people worked together for the common good." Today, employees are called partners because they are. It is no empty slogan.

This idea of partnership is demonstrated in other ways. In 1972, Lowe started a series of breakfast meetings in his home, to allow all employees over time to join in defining the core values of the company. This is hierarchy turned on its side. All the partners are involved in defining the values that would provide them a sense of meaning and purpose. This is a practice of leadership that elicits spirit, that gives life and energy to individuals and the organization.

Hierarchy is turned on its side in other ways at TDI. There are no private offices for executives, no special perks for those in positions of authority. To be sure, TDIndustries has hierarchy. It has executives. But it is not the executives who are celebrated. The first and last room people see as they arrive and leave the company is the Oak Room, with its pictures of whichever partners are currently celebrating anniversaries with the company.

TDIndustries emphasizes relationships and community. The partners still use the metaphor of family to describe their relationship. Jack Lowe Jr., son of the founder, says: "It is family. But it is more like brothers and sisters, not parents and children." Even this simple metaphor helps sustain spirit.

The importance of spirit is acknowledged, and the presence of spirit is experienced at TDI—within individuals, in relationships, and in the entire company or community. There is a link between leadership and spirit.

Spirited and Dispirited

Spirit matters. There is a contrast in spirit—the energy, the animation, the enthusiasm—between the people of Composite Corporation and the partners at TDIndustries. Here are some of the differences.

Spirited	Dispirited
Use all four energies (mental, physical, emotional, spiritual) at work	Use physical and mental at work
Work is vocation	Work is job
Sense of connectedness to others; community or family used as metaphor	Sense of separation and disconnectedness; more competition than cooperation and community
Congruence between personal and organizational mission and values; work has meaning and purpose	Lack of congruence between personal and organizational mission and values; lack of meaning and purpose
Energized, animated workers	Workers drained of energy
Workers involved in the activity of leadership	Leadership exercised in a top-down way

If spirit is always part of us, and if it is so important to our search for meaning and purpose, why do we experience it so seldom? What is it that constrains our awareness of spirit, in life and in work?

Many of the constraints are internal. Our drive to hurry up, to complete one task or activity so that we can move to another, keeps us from centering in the present and being open to the movement of spirit. Recall the lesson Sue Bender learned during her time with the Amish. I have learned and relearned it many times. I catch myself hurrying through lunch so that I can finish a letter and return several calls before going to my next meeting. I do it so I won't have to take work home so that I will have time to relax, only to find that there are other unfinished projects awaiting me at home. I am reminded of this pattern every time I receive "Speedbumps," a fun and insightful newsletter written by a friend who named it that because "all of us need speedbumps in our life to force us to slow down and pay attention."

We constrain the spirit if our workaholism is a true addiction. Too often, we use work to structure time because of our fear of emptiness and loneliness. Work is not a source of meaning, but a way of covering up the hard reality that our lives are void of purpose.

We constrain the spirit if we become so goal-oriented that we cannot enjoy the experience of doing (as opposed to the exhilaration of "having done"), if the destination is more important than the journey. Watching the hoopla surrounding the Super Bowl this past year, I was struck that it is not enough for a team to reach the pinnacle of the sport; it only matters that they win. The experience is not important; being victorious is. Likewise, being happy and content in one's present job is not enough; we must always be positioning ourselves to win, to get the next promotion or to reach the apex of the organizational pyramid. We constrain spirit if we get too attached to outcomes.

We constrain spirit if we don't act congruently, if our internal truth doesn't match our external behavior. We constrain spirit through our compulsions and through trying too hard to maintain too much control. As one of the twelve-step programs reminds us, we need to wear the world like a loose garment. We constrain the spirit with dogma.

We constrain the spirit if we live only in the external world, the world known through our five senses, the world of data and facts, the world of cash flows and bottom lines, the world in which we use mental and physical energy but not much else. Our environment invites us to live in this external world—the supposed "real world"—and we accept the invitation. But in doing so, we shut ourselves off from truths about ourselves, and ourselves in connection to others.

All of these constraints are important; we never fully experience the full presence of that unseen force called spirit unless we deal with them. But the constraint on spirit that is the focus of this book is how leadership is often understood and practiced.

In fact, spirit can and does weave through and enliven our understandings and practices of leadership, just as it weaves through and enlivens relationships. There is something different about I-thou relationships, about genuine partnerships, about relationships that are truly collaborative. This something different can be found in activities of leadership.

But it isn't always found there. A central tenet of this book is that some practices of leadership stifle spirit, or suffocate it altogether. In the next chapter, we turn our attention to the practices of leadership that are dispiriting. Then, in Chapter Four, I offer another way of understanding and practicing leadership, one that weaves together leadership and spirit.

Chapter Three

Leadership That Constrains Spirit

We do not call forth the best from people,
including ourselves, by naked force, by threat, by
subtle manipulation.

> —*Peter Vaill (1998, p. 195)*

Organizations that rely on chain of command
encourage unproductive, self-serving kinds of
communication. People in hierarchical
organizations almost invariably struggle for the
favor of those in power.

> —*Gifford Pinchot (1998, p. 43)*

How we typically understand and practice leadership has unintended consequences. We practice leadership in ways we have been taught, by example and in classes, and often we unwittingly suffocate spirit.

Three Vignettes

Martha was a high-potential manager working for the largest employer in her hometown. She ran one of the important units in her company, and she ran it with skill and aplomb. Her clients saw her as approachable and accessible, willing and able to listen, responsive to their needs. She related to her direct reports as thous, not its, building relationships with them based on respect and honor.

Even her superiors saw Martha as an exceptional performer; they selected her as the outstanding manager in the organization.

Midway through the next year, Martha was called in by a superior and told that she was being reassigned to manage another unit in another part of the city. There was no conversation about how a move might fit her career goals, and no consideration of her desires. Telling me this story, she said she was given time to ask just two questions: "Do I have a choice?" and "Are you trying to get me to retire?" The answer to both was no.

Martha also told me that she did not want the new assignment. She was energized by the work she was doing in her present organization, she was enjoying the relationships she had worked so hard to build, and she had unfinished work that she wanted to complete. But she had no choice. The decision had been made. The organizational leaders were convinced that they had made the right decision for the right reason. Their decision was imposed.

Martha went to the new unit and worked hard in her new job for almost a year. But she realized that she was not giving all of her energy to her work. She used mental and physical energy, she worked long hours and did more than what was required, but her spirit just wasn't in it. The decision-making process that placed her in this new job left her drained and dispirited. So she resigned. Now she is on the faculty of a local college, once again excited and energized by her work. A superb, gifted manager, she is no longer with the organization in which she made significant contributions and showed so much promise. She is no longer there because of how leadership was practiced.

Robbie is a brand manager in a large manufacturing organization. I have known him for several years. I describe him as knowledgeable, hardworking, focused, optimistic, considerate, and sensitive. He is a quick study. Once a problem is identified, he is very effective at identifying the underlying causes; he works effectively with others to spot the best solution and implement it. He is responsible and accountable.

One day, Robbie called. I could tell from the sound of his voice that his upbeat attitude was gone. As I listened, I could imagine him sitting at his desk, shoulders slumped, eyes downcast, feeling tired. The story he told was a simple one—so simple that it would be easy to dismiss it as insignificant.

He had just finished a hallway conversation with his boss, a senior executive with the company. They discussed the problems they were having with the final development and launch of an important new product. The executive not only expressed appropriate concern about the delay but then told Robbie exactly what needed to be done to get the product back on a fast track. Robbie knew from long experience that what the boss told him to do would not work, but he was upset and said he was going to do it anyway.

Robbie told me that he wished the executive had done just two small things differently. First, before giving an order the boss could have asked him what he thought needed to be done. Then, the boss could have asked if there was anything that he, the boss, could do to be of help. The boss, unintentionally, was practicing leadership in a way that left Robbie feeling dispirited.

Ruth was a bright and gifted human resource manager for a large multinational company. She received her first promotion to a managerial position and her first expatriate assignment. Becoming a manager and working abroad are challenging enough, but two other factors compounded the new assignment: her predecessor had failed at it, and one of Ruth's new direct reports felt that he should have been given the job she was moving into. She would be closely watched. The stakes were high, and the possibility of failure was real. With all of this going on, Ruth was excited—but even more, she was apprehensive about her move.

During the first week on her new job, an executive vice president called her into his office for what turned out to be a very brief conversation. He said, "I'm line, you're staff. As long as you work here, you do what I want. Understand?" Too unnerved to think clearly, Ruth simply acknowledged that she understood.

There were no words of welcome. No getting to know her. No word of encouragement. No offer of help or support. Not even communication of reasonable expectations. Just a quick and simple message that made it clear to Ruth that the EVP was boss. The downside is equally clear and simple: she went on to live in fear of the executive. She simply could not give all her energies to her work, or be the best she could be, while she was fearful of one of the executives who was to be an important client. The EVP might get Ruth's compliance; but with his style of leadership he could not get her commitment.

The Common Threads

Several themes run through these three vignettes.

In each story, and in each organization represented, the words *leader* and *executive* are used interchangeably. An executive is by definition an organizational leader, and the leader is an executive. Leader is defined by formal role in the organization more than by anything else. This is the executive-as-leader model that prevails today.

The organizational leaders portrayed in these vignettes were doing their job as we usually understand it. They were giving direction, taking charge, being forceful, allocating resources, delegating work. Because each was riding in a "higher helicopter"—seeing things from a greater altitude than the subordinates—each thought he had a better perspective on what the organization needed. In each case, the leader thought he was doing what needed to be done to serve the needs of the organization.

In each vignette, leadership was exercised in a command-and-control way. Direction was top-down. The leaders used coercive power to get what they wanted and what the organization ostensibly needed.

One other thread is important: these incidents, and the ones that you and I find dispiriting, happen in the normal day-to-day work of the organization. Spirit is not always knocked out of us by a huge punch thrown our way; small jabs can do the trick. From one perspective, the vignettes described above might seem rather insignificant, but from another that is exactly the point. One primary way that individuals lose touch with spirit is to be treated as an it in their everyday experiences at work.

A Brief History of Leadership Concepts

The behaviors of the so-called leaders in these vignettes, and of other like-minded executives, is rooted in an understanding of leadership that has evolved from research and practice. Our historic understanding has focused on the individual as leader, has used *leader* and *executive* interchangeably, and has invested in those individuals enormous power and authority.

From the earliest part of this century to the 1940s, the study of leadership focused on the qualities or traits that made individuals leaders. It was during this period that the "great man theory" of leadership was developed. The attributes of the great man included above-average intelligence, a tendency toward dominance, and an extroverted orientation toward life.

It was assumed that these attributes were the result of nature, not nurture; they were stable rather than changeable and would stand the leader in good stead regardless of the circumstance. Understood in this way, they preclude any of us *choosing* to become leaders; we are either born with leadership ability or we are out of luck.

The great-man theory of leadership is alive and well in some quarters today. When asked to think of great leaders, some people still think of men—a great president like Abraham Lincoln, a great general like George Patton, an outstanding coach like Vince Lombardi, or a captain of business and industry like Alfred P. Sloan. We still think of leaders as individuals who are larger than life, people who have traits that make them ideal. We want our leaders to be heroic, to be without fault, to be more than mere mortals. We continue to be disappointed whenever our heroes turn out to have feet of clay.

We see the effects of a version of the great-man theory in those organizations that focus on selecting leaders rather than developing them. We think that if we go to the right MBA schools and find the right persons, those with just the right traits, the cream will rise to the top. We don't want to *manufacture* cream; in fact, we see no need to. We can buy cream at the finest MBA schools or from other companies.

After this historic period of focusing on traits, we began to study the various behaviors or attributes of leaders. We studied the skills and abilities that leaders needed to exercise if they are to perform well. Some of the best-known studies were done at Ohio State, and from them we learned that effective leaders demonstrate both "task" behaviors (focused on accomplishing the work) and "maintenance" behaviors (focused on building and maintaining important relationships). Our hope was—and is—to find individuals who can combine each equally, or at least be versatile enough to move from one to the other quickly. The focus in this phase of the history of leadership thought was on identifying individuals who were adept enough to be task-focused and maintenance-focused.

Soon we began to believe that the qualities needed in a leader were not simply within the individual; leaders and leadership effectiveness could only be understood in relationship to followers. Here the emphasis moves from the individual to a relationship. Gary Wills, in *Certain Trumpets*, says that "a leader whose qualities do not match those of potential followers is simply irrelevant" (1994, p. 15). It is not enough to have the right traits or engage in the right behaviors. Instead, we are engaging in leadership only when followers are mobilized and their motives and interests are satisfied. It is not enough for a leader of uncommon intelligence to create a vision; he or she must be able to articulate it compellingly, in a way that truly engages followers.

This view of leadership is also in vogue today. A leader is not a leader without followers who follow—or so the thinking goes. This understanding of leadership emphasizes the relationship, but leadership is still not understood as an activity embedded within the relationship. Indeed, leadership is still understood as the province of that special person who can build and maintain effective relationships with followers.

In the 1960s, Fred Fiedler, a professor at the University of Illinois, proposed a contingency model of leadership. Fiedler, and others after him, suggested that leadership effectiveness depended on three contingencies that differed with the situation: leader-member relationship, the task to be done, and the leader's position and power. Effective leaders, it is argued, adapt their behavior to the particular situation. No one set of behaviors is always appropriate or effective. Today, one adaptation of this understanding of leadership is popularly called "situational leadership." James O'Toole calls it an "it depends" view of leadership. There is no right or wrong way to lead; appropriate leader behavior depends on the situation, on the skills and abilities of the followers, and on the abilities of the leader. Appropriate leadership depends on the interaction of the contingencies. Should a leader empower others? It depends. Should a leader exercise command and control? It depends. But who makes the decision of which leadership behavior is appropriate? The leader. So we have an individual exercising command-and-control leadership if he or she believes the situation requires it.

Today, our understanding of leaders is firmly grounded in these leadership studies and practices of the past. Though the view has shifted somewhat across the years—from an exclusive focus on the individual as leader to a focus more on the relationship between leader and follower—three themes or patterns pervade these views and tie them together:

1. There is inherent in each of these understandings of leadership the view that leadership is the province or possession of an individual. It is the gifted individual who is the leader.

2. The leader is identified with level and formal role in an organization. *Executive* and *leader* have been used interchangeably; the focus has been on the executive-as-leader.

3. Through the years, there has been a decline in the power difference between leader and follower, but it still remains. Even in the situational leadership model, because it is the leader who decides whether or not to share power the leader still has power over followers.

We have occasionally examined the shortcomings of this view of executive-as-leader, but we have assumed that the problem was with the leader rather than with our understanding or practice. Nothing wrong with the view of individual-as-leader, we thought, but sometimes the wrong person is chosen for the position. In fact, there *are* problems with our understanding of the executive-as-leader, not the least of which is that it has embedded within it the seeds of leadership behaviors that constrain spirit (recall the closing of Chapter Two). It is to several of these problems that we now turn our attention.

The Problem of Coercive Power

Power is a dynamic that exists in every relationship. There is no way to escape it. But there is a real difference between the personal power that accrues to an individual because of his or her competence and expertise on the one hand, and on the other the kind of power that comes with the territory of executives-as-leaders who occupy a lofty perch in a hierarchical organization.

Executives-as-leaders have coercive power. They use it sometimes to a good end, sometimes not. Coercive power is defined as having "power over"—enough so that others can be forced into acting in a prescribed way. Coercive power is based on having something the other wants (a reward) or fears (a punishment). The reward can be a pay raise, promise of a promotion, an opportunity to present to senior executives, public recognition— anything the follower values and wants. Punishments also range from the severe to the subtle: from being fired to being given a less-than-challenging task.

Even senior-level leaders in hierarchical organizations who prefer not to use coercive power still have it. The ability to coerce is always there, explicitly or implicitly. Followers do not ignore or forget it. Coercive power used subtly or toward a beneficial end is still coercive; a benevolent dictator is still a dictator. Because organizational leaders in hierarchical organizations have the ability to exercise command and control (and a seeming mandate to command and control if the situation warrants), and because command and control requires the use of coercive power, it is important to understand the consequences of this practice of leadership.

Executives or managers who use coercive power get compliance, but not commitment. In the first of the vignettes described earlier, Martha moved to the new role she was assigned. She complied with the directive from her boss. She did the best she could, but she simply did not have spiritual energy to give to her work. Her boss could force her compliance but not command her commitment.

A command-and-control leadership style engenders resistance. Whenever coercive power flows one way in a relationship, hostility and resentment flow in the other. Sometimes the resistance is not seen; but it is there—it surfaces in the form of malicious obedience— doing what one is told even though it is clearly wrong. This is the case in Robbie's story. He was going to do what he was told, even though he knew it would not work. But sometimes the resistance surfaces in the form of open rebellion, retaliation, or fighting back. This kind of rebellion can be seen in all types of relationships; consider how children respond to autocratic parents and workers respond to autocratic bosses.

The use of coercive power encourages either dependency or fear on the part of workers. It is the only way coercive power can be maintained. With dependency comes avoidance of risk taking, behavior designed primarily to gain approval, decisions to tell the boss what he or she wants to hear. With fear comes lack of creativity, refusal to accept responsibility for behavior (and corresponding blaming and CYA, or "cover your ass," behaviors), and resorting to such attitudes as "I'm going to do exactly what I'm told to do, no more and no less." This is Ruth's story in the third vignette. She lived in fear of the executive vice president. She was careful to do only what she was told; going beyond that might trigger his anger.

Fear and dependency are particularly toxic companions of command-and-control practices of leadership, and of the related use of coercive power. They poison spirit, both that of the executive and that of the one being coerced.

But there is more. Command-and-control leadership practices encourage competition more than collaboration, promote consistency more than creativity, and discourage new ideas and innovative projects. This is what we saw in Martha, Robbie, and Ruth's stories.

Coercive power corrupts the executive at the same time that it is discouraging and dispiriting employees. Maintaining power over others slowly infects executives with an unhealthy sense of their own importance; the end result is often that they move from healthy regard of themselves, which is important, to unhealthy self-centeredness.

The use of coercive power withers spirit. Spirit, like commitment, cannot be coerced, cajoled, pressured, or threatened into being present. Spirit is an essential part of who we are; it is with us always no matter how faint or disguised. But it can become so withered by command-and-control practices of leadership that we lose touch with it. If we do, we also lose touch with a vital source of energy that enlivens us and keeps us going.

(Sometimes I wonder if the use of coercive power is essentially a "man thing." It does seem clear to me that men are conditioned to believe that every potentially competitive activity is a test of manhood. The learned response is to use force to prevail, to win. If work activities are viewed through a competitive lens—men seem to think that there will always be winners and losers—then coercive power is the secret weapon certain to ensure triumph.)

Command-and-Control Leadership: A Case Study

Until his recent retirement, Robert Crandall was the well-known chairman of American Airlines. He was an innovative and visionary leader. He made enormous contributions to American Airlines and to the industry. His ability to think and act strategically kept American a market leader. During his tenure, American became the industry leader in using technology—the Sabre system—to distribute tickets through travel agents. American was the first airline to reward loyal customers with frequent-flyer mileage. And American made money during his tenure. Crandall's leadership provided good returns to stockholders. As a leader he was resourceful, willing to do whatever it took to succeed; he persevered during times of turmoil caused by deregulation.

He was also a prototype of the command-and-control leader who uses coercive power. Often cited as one of America's toughest bosses, Crandall was hard-nosed and autocratic. He could be as inept in dealing with people as he was adept at dealing with other aspects of running a business.

On at least two occasions during the 1990s, Crandall got into public tiffs with American's flight attendants and pilots. The fights centered around strikes, or the possibility thereof, and even though these prospects themselves raise the ante and are emotion-laden, Crandall's public statements only made a difficult situation worse. The public spats clearly demonstrated the drawbacks of an autocratic, command-and-control leader who uses coercion in an attempt to get what he wants.

Several years ago, American created a two-tiered wage system, maintaining the roster of present pilots at existing salaries but hiring new pilots on a scale of greatly reduced salaries. With the growth of the industry in general, and American in particular, it wasn't too many years before the lower-paid pilots made up a majority of their union. So in 1997, Crandall and American Airlines were employing pilots who had been treated like second-class citizens, who were tired of feeling one-down, and who would get even in the only way available to them: going out on strike. On one level, it looks as if the strike was about wages and related issues; at another level, it was clear that a more basic issue was mistrust, the seeds of which had been sown several years earlier.

How did Crandall respond to the possibility of a strike? With threats. At one point he told pilots he would get out of the passenger-service business if they did not accept American's position. How did the pilots respond to the threat? With resentment. As suggested earlier, whenever coercive power flows one way in a relationship, resentment flows in the other.

In 1993, before the most recent strike, American Airline pilots presented Crandall with the results of a study that showed new ways American could use its fleet more efficiently, thus reducing costs without having an impact on pay scales. In a meeting with analysts, Crandall demeaned their ideas. "If the pilots were in charge," he said, "Columbus would still be in port. They believe the assertion that the world is flat" (Purdum, 1997, p. C22). The pilots' response to this demeaning behavior was predictable: they met it with hostility and determination to get even.

The story of Robert Crandall and the pilots and attendants of American Airlines is a dramatic example of the consequences of using coercive power. In other organizations the details might change, the story might not play out on center stage, and the use of coercive power might be far more subtle, but the dynamics are the same. Employees respond to leaders who use coercive power by fighting back openly or underhandedly, by taking flight (ignoring the boss or leaving the company), or by submitting or complying.

But one other implication here is at the heart of this book: individuals do not use all of their energies at work, do not operate on the best they have within them, and are not as enthusiastic or energized (both fruits of the spirit) by their work if leadership is characterized by command and control and the related use of coercive power. Fear is one of the dark sides of coercive power, and we don't experience spirit when we live in fear.

The presence and use of coercive power by executives-as-leaders is a primary reason it is hard to use this practice of leadership in a way that elicits spirit. Indeed, it is in large part because of the use of coercive power that organizations get the opposite: half-hearted, unenthusiastic, uninspired performance.

The Dark Side of Executives

A second reason it is hard to get inspired, committed performance from executive-as-leader practices of leadership is that the executive's shadow gets in the way.

Carl Jung, the Swiss psychologist, made vast contributions to our understanding of the human psyche. He developed a complex understanding of personality, of which the concept of shadow (and related to it the concept of persona) was a part. Our persona is the part of us we make public, the face we wear for society. Our persona is shaped by the same forces that help shape our identity: childhood conditioning, our culture, the jobs we have, our socioeconomic status. Each of us has a general persona that the world sees. But we can also change the face we show—the mask we put on—to fit the situation.

Our public self has a partner who is less visible, one we try to hide from the public, one who exists outside the light of day: our shadow. The shadow is full of those things we have no wish to be, and certainly no wish to present to the public: our fears, our insecurities, our anxieties. Jung said, "everyone carries a shadow and the less it is embodied in a person's conscious life, the blacker and denser it is . . . shadow is not evil, just somewhat inferior, primitive, and unadapted. It even contains childlike qualities which would in a way vitalize and embellish human existence" (Jacobi, 1973, p. 113).

So much has been written about former presidents of the United States that the persona they make public and their shadow are often well known. The persona of Richard Nixon, the part of himself he wanted to project, was the cool, thoughtful, forceful, progressive president, moving the United States out of Vietnam and opening up trade with China. This is largely what we saw of him. What we did not see so well was the fear, anger, and vengeful nature that only later showed up on tapes not made for public consumption. For Nixon, as for all of us, there was a great split between his persona and his shadow.

The shadow is not something that executives talk about, not even something that most acknowledge. Instead, executives live essentially in an external world. Their jobs require it, and they prefer it. Executives deal with the so-called real world of data known to the senses, with hard numbers and tough problems, with deadlines and bottom lines. They even deal with the external reality of people, with behaviors that can be observed, rather than with thoughts and feelings and spirit, all of which are internal and seemingly off-limits.

Schools, and particularly MBA programs, do an admirable job of teaching future managers and executives to live in this world of externals. They learn to analyze, organize, plan, identify and solve problems, budget, and act strategically. They leave the formal education process with great ability to handle anything that can be quantified. Then they enter the world of organizations, where those who can best navigate the fast currents and occasional eddies of permanent white water are rewarded and reinforced. Influence and power accrue to them. This emphasis on the external world encourages individuals to pay attention to their persona, the face they wear in public.

Executives—and the rest of us, for that matter—typically know little about their shadow. Nowhere in the formal education process are they encouraged to go down and in, to discover what's going on deep inside. Few leadership-development programs encourage executives to deal with their inner life, with what's going on in their depths. To borrow a phrase from writer Frederick Buechner, they deal more with their "shallows" than their "depths." Day-to-day life in the corporation leaves little time for reflection and introspection. Executives mainly don't think of the inner life as the right stuff to deal with. So individual executives-as-leaders deny the shadow exists ("What you see is what you get"); they ignore it, or more likely they project it onto their environment.

The problem is that the shadow cannot be ignored. As much as we wish it weren't true, whatever is buried deep inside (truths about us that are not fully part of our awareness) pop up to haunt us, and they do so at all the wrong times. We project what's going on in our shadow onto relationships, into the decisions we make, into the exercise of leadership. What goes on deep within drives us, but often in ways we don't fully understand. "I am afraid that we may feed a common delusion among leaders," says Parker Palmer, "that their efforts are always well intended, their power always benign. I suggest that the challenge is to examine our consciousness for those ways in which leaders may project more shadow than light" (1998b, p. 5).

In recent years, I have had the opportunity to work with many executives-as-leaders who had a leadership style that seemed driven from something deep within; none of them seemed to know it. They projected a lot of shadow.

One of these executives had been a chief executive in several different organizations when I met him. He had enjoyed successes and suffered failures in all three. The successes he deserved. He possessed a towering intellect, enormous courage, an expansive personality, and great charm. Part of his charm was related to his storytelling ability. He could warm even the most resistant of audiences with his ability to weave a story. But his failures were also deserved. He was an anger-based person. He was emotionally volatile and unpredictable. He could turn from warm and charming to angry in a split second. When he did so, he used his intellect to slice and dice people. All of us get angry at times, but his anger was different. It was pervasive. It was always there, lurking just beneath the surface. Too many of his actions, including his leadership actions, were based on it. Though I do not know the source of his anger, my hunch is that it comes from his depths. It is part of his shadow. He seemed to know his anger was a problem, but he was not willing to go down and in to discover the deep source of it. The problem, of course, is that the anger popped up at the wrong time, haunted him, and hurt others.

A second leader, who was acting as a CEO when I worked with him, is fear-based. Interestingly, it is hard to see the fear. A man's man, he loves to hunt, and he displays his hunting trophies throughout his house. He appears extremely self-confident. He is a political animal; he smells things that are going to be successful and positions himself in the center of the action, and he carefully distances himself from things that could be trouble. His fear becomes obvious in his attempts to control. He orders meetings in his organization audiotaped so he can know what his subordinates are saying. He won't allow his direct reports, all senior executives, to speak for the organization. He even carefully monitors the information given to his board. The fear infects him, and it infects the women and men of his organization. Not surprisingly, one word these executives uses to describe him is "paranoid." In truth, though, the organization is also full of fear, and even paranoia; the malaise is projected by the leader onto the organization. The fear is deeply rooted within this leader; it is part of his shadow. I know him fairly well, though, and he has never acknowledged his fearfulness. He has done so well living in the external world and enjoys all the trappings of success (as we typically define it) that he has felt no need to go inside and discover the source of this fear.

Yet another leader with whom I have worked was so driven by his need to please others that it affected everything he said and did. He was one of the warmest, nicest people you could ever meet. He was enabling, encouraging, and empowering. He listened well. He involved people in making decisions. But you could never be sure the decisions you agreed on would stick, because in his next meeting with his higher-ups his need to please them would lead him to say what they wanted to hear rather than to argue for the decision you had agreed on. He did not intend to speak out of both sides of his mouth; he just had such a strong need to please others that he did it without really being aware of it. He also had a tough time being forceful, confronting difficult problems, holding conflict, making hard decisions. Being forceful might cost him the approval and affirmation he craved, or so he thought. Like the other two executives I've described, his need for affirmation seemed to be driven by something deep within, something outside his conscious awareness.

Being driven by a need for approval, as this third executive was, is an example of being driven by a dependency need. Executives are a mixture of autonomies and dependencies, but it is the autonomous side that executives think is good and want others to see—the ability to stand on one's own two feet, to make independent judgments, to be capable of handling the responsibilities, to be self-sufficient. These are part of the executive's persona. Dependency needs—need for recognition and approval, for safety, or, as the third leader's story relates, for affection or affirmation—usually remain in the unconscious or hidden in the shadow. By and large, executives would feel too vulnerable to let these needs surface, so they try to repress them, or they project them onto others in the workplace.

Other aspects of the shadow that pop up to haunt executives-as-leaders include the fears and insecurities that are at least partially buried deep within, the prejudices that are not part of their awareness, the ways they hate themselves that get projected onto others, their deep-down belief that people cannot be trusted. To the extent that these dynamics remain part of an unexamined life, they keep executives from being fully human, fully authentic, and fully effective in leadership roles. Let me say it more clearly: none of us can be fully effective in leadership activities unless we have done deep inner work, unless we have gone down and in and embraced our shadow.

There is an important link between the shadow side of executives-as-leaders and the use of coercive power. The anger-based leader uses command-and-control leadership practices even when the situation does not require it. He or she does not think about what leadership style is needed or would be most effective but instead reacts to the anger that is within by bullying others. Likewise for fear-based and insecurity-based leaders. Their choice of leadership style is not based on a rational and careful look at the situation; instead, they are driven by their unexamined needs to exercise command and control.

The question remains: if shadow is part of each of us, then why single out the executive-as-leader for special attention? Doesn't each of us project our shadow into our environment, including those times when we are involved in the activity of leadership? The answers are that we each have a shadow, and yes, we each project it into our leadership activities. But, just as a tall building casts a longer shadow than a short one, because of an executive's place in the hierarchy he or she casts a longer shadow. An executive simply has an unusual degree of influence or power to create the conditions under which others must work. If the executive projects more shadow than light, he or she creates dark conditions for others in the organization. Without conscious planning or any intent that it happen, organizations become the repository of the executive-as-leader's shadow; the shadow is then reflected in obvious ways, even if it is not recognized as shadow.

So long as we define leaders as individuals and persist in equating leadership with roles in organizations, and so long as executives continue to perform with their inner lives unexamined, their shadow goes on creating dark corners in the world of work. If executives do not know what it is deep within that drives them, they continue their anger-based, fear-based, approval-based, or insecurity-based practices of leadership. The impact on others, and on the organization, is costly.

One of the costs is to spirit. Spirit, the unseen force that infuses and energizes, that gives us energy and life, gets covered up in individuals and organizations in which the executive-as-leader casts a large shadow.

The Problem of Ego

A healthy ego is important to individuals. We need a strong sense of self; we need to understand ourselves as individuals, separate and distinct from others. In everyday conversation, it seems as though having an *ego* is a negative condition. To the contrary, any individual who is going to participate effectively in the activity of leadership, or engage fully in the life process, needs a strong and healthy ego.

Executives-as-leaders must have a full measure of self-confidence; they must believe in their capabilities to perform in high-pressure situations. They must not be riddled with self-doubt. Having self-confidence and the resilience to bounce back from tough situations is called ego strength; it is a necessary prerequisite for being a successful executive.

But when does a strong sense of self become self-centeredness? When does healthy self-confidence become arrogance? "However fine the line," suggests Bob Kaplan, "when a manager goes from having self-confidence to having a big ego, there are serious consequences, not only for that person's performance, but also for his or her ability to learn from experience" (1991, p. 39).

Men and women with big egos, driven by a personal need for power and status, strive for positions of power and authority; thus individuals with big egos are found rather often in the position of executive-as-leader. The trip up the organizational ladder is intoxicating, encouraging big egos to get bigger. Every rung on the ladder provides an increasing array of perks, from special parking places to private bathrooms, from fortresslike executive suites to fortune-making bonus plans. The ascent pushes those who start with a lot of self-confidence and ego strength toward (if not over) the line that separates self-confidence from arrogance, and it often changes those who start out determined to keep their ego in check. Executives easily fall victim to an inflated ego.

The environment in the executive suite encourages occupants to live with the illusion of their own importance, and the importance of their ideas; simultaneously, it devalues the ideas and opinions of others. The physical environment usually isolates executives from criticism. Not only are their offices usually physically separate but executives don't invite criticism or make it at all easy for others to give it. The power difference between leader and follower, and the problem so many of us have with authority figures, makes it difficult for employees to be honest—or even to offer alternative viewpoints, should they be invited to do so. In this environment, it is easy for executives to develop an exalted sense of their self-worth.

Being an executive is heady stuff, and in the environment in which executives live it is hard for them not to feel special. It is an easy step to feel and act as if rules that govern normal conduct do not apply (even with something so simple as a policy that no one in the company flies first class—except, of course, the executives, who are different and therefore deserve more comfort). It is easy to become self-centered. Like Narcissus of Greek legend, executives begin to fall in love with their image.

One of the senior management teams with which I have worked in recent years comprises seven men, all close to forty, all but one formally identified as high-potential, all ambitious, and all full of ego. There is a stark difference between the way they talk about themselves as a team (what Chris Argyris called their "espoused theory") and the way they actually function (their "theory in practice"). They describe themselves as a well-functioning team, one with a lot of camaraderie and little conflict, and with a shared belief that the company's well-being is of primary concern. But in their team meetings they talk past each other, don't seem open to viewpoints other than their own, and work harder to protect their turf than they do to consider the corporate good. Away from the meeting, they are openly critical of each other. As I observe these men, I wonder if the crown prince syndrome also applies to nonroyalty, those corporate figures identified as high-potential, encouraging those who have healthy egos to develop an inflated sense of self.

There is also a problem if the executive-as-leader has a weak ego. Executives who think of themselves as powerless or irrelevant, who act from a deep-down feeling of worthlessness and insecurity, are going to project their insecurity onto the organization and use coercive power in attempts to cover it. In this environment, it is easy for employees to see themselves in terms of I-it, as tools or pawns (in today's parlance, as human assets), being used instrumentally to meet the needs of high-level executives. Under these circumstances it is difficult, if not impossible, for employees to give the best they have to their work, to act with spiritual energy, to see themselves as partners in making the business a success.

Tilted Toward the Problems?

You might take what I have written about executives as too damning, focused too much on the problems of the executive-as-leader and not enough on the obvious successes many executives have earned as well as the high esteem in which they are held.

I am deeply impressed with most of the executives-as-leaders whom I have known and with whom I have been privileged to work. They are, as a group, bright, energetic, gifted men and women. They work incredibly hard, often making real sacrifices to advance their careers and their companies' fortunes. They are resourceful, decisive, and willing to do whatever it takes to get their agenda completed. Most care deeply about people and about doing the right thing.

But executives shape, and are shaped by, the environment in which they work. As I have tried to make clear, they would not be executives without an ego, but the environment in which they work tends to inflate it. Coercive power comes with the territory; executives have it whether they want it or not. The dark side is evident because executives always cast shadows, and (as I have said) the larger-than-life the executive, the larger the shadow. Very few executives have intentionally worked on the inner life to bring the internal forces of ego, power, and shadow into the light.

I have focused on the problems as a way of making the point that the concept of executive-as-leader has embedded within it consequences that make the concept no longer as viable as perhaps it once was. It is not the men and women who are bad or wrong (even though some may be); rather, it is the idea of executive-as-leader whose time is past—or at least is passing.

One reason the concept of executive-as-leader hasn't passed more quickly is that those of us who are followers have believed in the concept and thus supported its continuation. If a new model of leadership is to emerge, followers must stop encouraging leaders to act in ways we say we don't want.

Owning Our Responsibility:
How We Collude with Executives-as-Leaders

One reason that heroic, command-and-control leaders with coercive power and inflated egos have stayed so long in vogue is collusion. It is a central problem with which we must wrestle if we are to move beyond our present understanding and practice of leadership. To collude is to conspire, to engage in secret agreements and behaviors that run counter to what we say publicly that we want and will do. For example, we say we want to be involved in the activity of leadership, but secretly what we want is for our organization to have at the top leaders who are strong, wise, honest, fair, and farsighted—in a word, ideal. We say we want autonomy and control, but really what we want is for someone else to be in control, to be responsible and accountable, and we want them to be consistent and benevolent, like a good father or mother. Our role is to follow, to be good children. For the most part, we know what it means to follow: to heed direction, to use the chain of command, to show respect, to be loyal. Though we don't usually say it out loud, we are willing to give up a sense of ownership, of being part of the leadership process, as long as the leader provides us safety and security. This is the deal, implicitly agreed to. This is collusion.

In organization after organization, workgroup after workgroup, one reason that empowerment has not worked is that we, the men and women of the organization, don't want it. We want more control, but we don't want the accountability. We want to take potshots at the leaders and the dumb things they do, but we resist their invitation to be involved in making things better. We are ambivalent men and women. Peter Block says it well: "We want to go to heaven, but we don't want to die" (1993, p. 39).

In a large telecommunications company, one manager worked hard to turn a small, well-defined group into a self-managing team. The manager knew that traditional hierarchy and coercive power were not getting the best results. He wanted the group to be empowered and act it. He worked hard to move from a hierarchical workgroup to a community. He engaged the members in dialogue about the possibilities, he managed disagreements nicely, and he knew he could not create a new way of doing work by command and control. He gave team members options in managing the flow of the work, delegating it, solving problems, and disciplining team members. From the very outset, the members were not sure they liked the idea. It was too threatening. It didn't feel safe. In the end, they decided to keep things as they were. A new window of opportunity had been opened and a new breeze blew in, but the members of the workgroup chose to shut the window. In doing so, they walked away from an opportunity for shared leadership and an environment that fostered growth of spirit.

This is but one example of how we collude with executives-as-leaders who use command-and-control leadership techniques. Here are two others I often observe.

We Say Yes When We Want to Say No

We don't speak our truth when the executive-as-leader is making a decision with which we disagree or is acting in a way we think is wrong. This is exactly the reason so many workgroups and organizations "go to Abilene." *The Abilene Paradox* is the story told by Jerry Harvey (1998) of a decision made in his wife's family, with Harvey as a participant, to drive from Coleman, Texas, to Abilene on a sweltering hot August day to eat in a cafeteria, only to learn on the return trip that nobody really want to go but each person had agreed to just to please the others. "Going to Abilene" has entered our lexicon as a way of talking about the collusion that happens in workgroups and organizations when we say yes while wanting to say no.

We Relate to Organizational Leaders out of Fear or Dependency

It is ironic, but true: leaders who use coercive power can only do so if we let them, if we are afraid of any punishment they might mete out, or if we are dependent on them for a reward they might give. Coercive power is not something an organizational leader has; we give them power over us because of our fears or dependency needs. We stop colluding only if we are willing to struggle with our own inner issues with authority figures and decide not to let others have power over us. To be sure, this is not easy. External and internal pressures often encourage us to stay in dependent, one-down positions. But staying in a one-down position withers spirit, and it does not allow us to move to a new understanding and practice of leadership in which all of our energies are needed and can be used.

The flip side of collusion is courage: to be authentic, to act with integrity, to speak our truth. Collusion takes energy from us and withers spirit. Being courageous gives us energy and honors spirit. But being courageous is not easy; deciding to act courageously is often a tough choice to make. Sometimes feedback is not welcomed, and honesty is punished. Sometimes the reason we collude is not because of cowardice, but because we know that speaking up has negative consequences. There are other times when we might safely speak up but choose not to; we choose collusion over courage. Life in organizations is full of moral ambiguities, and the question of when to speak up and when to keep silent, when to accommodate and when to push back, is not easily decided.

A Different Practice of Leadership

I have mentioned three of the most important problems with the prevailing top-down, command-and-control, executive-as-leader model: the use of coercive power, the problem of the executive's dark side, and the problems related to ego. But there are also positive forces, positive reasons, to consider a new understanding and practice of leadership.

The Changing Nature of Work and Workers

Several trends combine to make today's worker very different from his or her predecessor. A growing number of workers are employed by outsourcing firms rather than by the company for whom they are working. Others are employed by the company but on a "contract" basis. These phenomena are examples of the new employment contract, which means, in effect, that organizations no longer promise lifetime employment but instead offer work on a project-by-project basis. One unintended consequence is the growing number of individuals who no longer fear the "highway." As you and I give up the fear of losing our jobs, we reclaim our personal power. Peter Drucker says this means workers today have to be treated as if they are volunteers.

Then there are more and more men and women today who are knowledge workers, individuals who know more about their work than their boss does. This simple fact impacts our understanding and practice of leadership. Warren Bennis says that "to a large degree our growing recognition for the need for a new, more collaborative form of leadership results from the emergence of intellectual capital as the most important element of organizational success" (1997, p. 84). Knowledge workers can easily sabotage autocratic bosses who try to use coercive power.

The Increasing Diversity of the Workforce

Workforce 2000, and other studies like it, have clearly shown that the demographics of the workforce are changing, and changing quickly (Johnston, 1987). Women and minorities will soon be the majority of workers. They bring with them unaccustomed hopes and expectations about leadership.

The approach to leadership that suggests an executive-as-leader can create a vision and develop a sense of purpose that is shared by all (and that gains their commitment) is no longer viable. This might have been the case back when the workforce was more homogeneous, when workers were more similar than dissimilar in their backgrounds, values, and expectations; but in the much more heterogeneous workplace it is simply not possible for an executive-as-leader, no matter how farsighted or how aware of the differing needs of workers, to articulate a vision and mission that is readily shared. What is needed is a practice of leadership that honors diversity of viewpoints and uses that diversity to develop a shared sense of meaning and purpose.

The Increasing Complexity of Tasks and Technology

Ever-more-complex tasks and technology are calling for a new understanding and practice of leadership. Organizations now realize that if work is going to be done effectively, there must be integration across specialized functions and activities. Expertise must be widely shared; individuals *and* organizations must learn. Tasks can no longer be efficiently or successfully completed with workers staying inside their stovepipes and protecting their turf. Stovepipes create barriers to the coordination and accomplishment of work; they leave little room for spirit.

By and large, stovepipes are the product of hierarchy. Hierarchy evolved as a way of getting work done efficiently, and it allowed easy administration of command and control. But it put people in boxes and separated functions. In a typical manufacturing environment, engineering is separated from production, which is separated from sales and marketing. In a hierarchy, coordination comes from the top.

In today's more complex environment a new type of cooperation—and coordination—is needed if tasks are to be accomplished effectively. Coordination needs to come from the side rather than the top. A current example of coordination from the side is the self-managing workteam. In these teams, there is often no executive-as-leader creating a vision, setting direction, allocating resources, or making decisions. The team is accountable for its work. Individuals participate in the activity of leadership.

Technologies that have emerged in recent years, e-mail and videoconferencing being notable examples, are nudging us—sometimes without our being aware of it—toward different practices of leadership. E-mail flattens organizations; now any employee can communicate with any other employee without using the chain of command. Videoconferencing allows individuals in dispersed locations to work together to set new directions, determine strategies, and solve complex problems—all acts of leadership.

Emphasis on Quality and Service Requires New Leadership Practices

To ensure quality and provide world-class customer service requires that leadership not be practiced in a top-down, command-and-control way. In many organizations, responsibility for exercising leadership is being pushed down to men and women on the front line, those who know and interact with the customer most closely. In schools it is called site-based management; in manufacturing environments it is giving the individual on the shop floor the right to stop the assembly line if a problem with quality is detected. To be sure, in some organizations empowerment is more a buzzword than a reality, and in others sharing the practice of leadership is happening in fits and starts. But it is happening. The line separating leader and follower is blurring. Organizations have learned that men and women cannot be energized and enthusiastic about their work if they have to get a dozen approvals to do what they know is best for the customer or the quality of the product.

Executives-as-leaders also need a new way of understanding leadership. The complexities of the task, the level of expertise needed, and (as noted earlier) the increasing sophistication of technology make it impossible for an individual executive to effectively exercise leadership. William Plamondon, president and CEO of

Budget Rent-a-Car, writes: "The cloak of leadership is heavy and needs to be shared. No one person can lead or energize an organization. As more people become leaders, the organization will be able to grow, respond, and move faster and faster, thus creating more energy" (1996, pp. 278–279).

The Need to Get the Best from the People of the Organization

Too often, the executive-as-leader model does not call forth the best that people have within them, does not encourage them to commit all of their energies to their work, does not elicit commitment and passion. In a competitive environment, organizations cannot afford full-headed but half-hearted workers.

It is time for a better understanding and practice of leadership. It is time to rethink even our most basic of assumptions of what leadership is and who leaders are. It is time to develop a way of doing leadership that engages all the energies of all the people—including their spiritual energy—in service of their work.

Chapter Four

An Inspiriting Alternative: Partnership

> Work is about the search for daily meaning as well
> as daily bread, for recognition as well as for cash,
> for astonishment rather than torpor; in short, for
> a sort of life rather than a Monday through Friday
> sort of dying.
>
> *—Studs Terkel (1974, p. xi)*

If the idea of executive-as-leader has outlived its usefulness, what is to replace it? What practice of leadership elicits inspired, enthusiastic performance? What kind of leadership encourages men and women in organizations to be the best they can be, to use all of their energies in the service of their work? If command-and-control leaders stifle spirit, what understanding and practice of leadership is inspiriting?

To repeat, leadership has been predominantly understood as something an individual provides. Leaders lead. They provide a compelling vision. They set direction and determine strategy. They make key decisions. They motivate and inspire. This is the industrial model, the executive-as-leader practice of leadership.

We have tried everything we know to make this model work more effectively. Executives are constantly offered a new leadership theory du jour, each one promising to make them more effective. They have been offered techniques and models, listened to countless speeches and multimedia presentations, and used personal coaches and classroom training to help the executive-as-leader be effective.

We have assumed that this understanding and practice is a good one and that our task is simply to do it better. It is time, though, to try another way of understanding and practicing leadership.

A Different Understanding and Practice: Partnership

Here's an alternative: understanding and practicing leadership as *partnership*. The idea of partnership suggests the basic concept of two or more people sharing power and joining forces to move toward accomplishment of a shared goal. It is understanding that leadership is an activity that happens in and comes from a collective—sometimes two people, sometimes more.

In this alternative view, leadership is not something that one individual provides to another. It is not the province of an individual, but rather something that results from the *reciprocity of relationships*. It is "a distributed process shared by many ordinary people instead of the expression of a single extraordinary individual" (Drath, 1998, p. 404).

The very definition of partnership suggests a relationship where people are equals. Not one leader and many followers; not one person giving orders and others taking them; not one-up, one-down. Instead, leadership is cocreated; individuals relate as partners and create a shared vision, set direction, solve ambiguous and tough problems, and find meaning in their work.

Partnerships also suggest interdependence, a blending of dependent and independent behaviors. They reveal a way to meet the human needs that were described in the first chapter: each of us needs to individuate and to have our own identity, and we need to experience connectedness and community. The understanding of leadership that suggests that it comes from an individual does not usually allow for interdependence; in fact, we often relate to the heroic leader from a stance of codependence or counterdependence. Partnerships require interdependence. When we act interdependently, we recognize the differing gifts, skills, and energies we each bring to any given leadership activity; we know we can do more together than alone, and we fully engage each other as partners to cocreate that something else.

I have been careful not to call this a *new* understanding of leadership because, in fact, partnership-as-leadership happens often:

- Kids in school use partnership-as-leadership as they organize themselves on the playground. Left to their own devices and with a bit of unstructured time, they create a game, agree on directions and roles, and manage the process—including the conflicts that often arise. Leadership is a shared activity.

- Community and neighborhood groups use partnerships as they spring up and organize themselves to tackle specific issues. Leadership results from the give and take of relationships. Even if a spokesperson emerges for these ad hoc groups, as is often the case, he or she emerges from the interaction of individuals rather than through a selection imposed on them. In ad hoc community groups, no one person has power over another. Power is shared among the partners in the process.

- Partnership also happens in corporate organizations. It can happen in a self-managed team of workers on the shop floor, or a senior executive team on the top floor. It happens when individuals act as partners to do the work of the organization and accomplish a shared goal.

Partnership-as-leadership is not a new practice, but we are so accustomed to executive-as-leader that when we see or experience partnership-as-leadership we don't consider it to be real leadership.

In partnerships, leadership is understood more as a verb than a noun. It is developing a shared sense of purpose. It is cocreating a vision and a mission statement. It is working together to make sense out of complex situations. It is holding conflict and honoring differences as we collaborate and cocreate a solution that works for all. The focus is on working interdependently, working as part of a collective, to accomplish a shared goal. In contrast, in the executive-as-leader practice of leadership the emphasis is on the noun: the leader.

Partnerships mitigate the issues of power, ego, and shadow that I addressed in the preceding chapter. Partnerships work when power is shared, when each person in the partnership claims his or her personal power and decides not to use coercive power even if it is available. In partnerships, ego is still important, but now the ego needs of each person are acknowledged and honored. As we do this, we minimize the chance that the inflated ego needs of a single person dominate. In true partnerships, egos are held somewhat in check. Likewise with shadow; each person involved in a partnership carries a shadow, and it can be projected onto the partnerships. But from the very nature of partnerships, the shadow projected by a single individual is less severe or painful. As we grow as individuals and learn to embrace our shadow, we lessen its negative impact even more.

In partnerships, leadership is not an outside-in process. It is not opening up another person's (the follower's) head or heart and filling it with truth or values or meaning that is external to the person. Leadership is not forcing alignment with an executive's vision. It is not requiring allegiance to goals that are not shared. It is not "them" doing something to or for "us."

Instead, in the partnership model leadership is an inside-out process. It comes from within individuals and from the relationships of which they are a part. It is surfacing the meaning and purpose that individuals and partners bring to their work and want from it. It is freeing individuals and groups to be the best they can be. All these things—a sense of meaning, a desire to be the best, a desire to use all of one's gifts and energies in the service of the work—exist within individuals. The purpose of the activity of leadership is to bring them to the surface, to bring them from the inside out.

Said another way, partnership is the activity that evokes and involves spirit. The process of partnership-as-leadership has the capacity to move us beyond the rational and logical, beyond the physical, beyond even the emotional, to the unseen force at the core of our being that defines who we are; that connects us to others; and that provides us, individually and collectively, with a sense of meaning.

The Five Requirements

There are five requirements for the partnership model to work.

Balance of Power

The partnership model does not work if one person or several people have power and others don't. The partnership model does not work if one person or one group uses positional or coercive power. Rather, the partnership model works whenever all individuals claim their personal power and use it to help cocreate win-win situations and reach a shared goal. As suggested in the last chapter, partnerships work well if we acknowledge and work with our shadow so that we can use our power appropriately. (More about power later in this chapter.)

Shared Purpose

There must be a shared sense of purpose, a shared goal. In a partnership, there are divergent opinions of how to reach a goal, but a shared understanding of the goal. There are differing tactics, but a shared sense of purpose. There are interpersonal disagreements and conflict—and it is important that partners learn to honor them—but underneath there is a shared commitment to a larger mission.

Shared Responsibility

There must be a shared sense of responsibility and accountability. Whether in a one-to-one relationship, a group, or a larger community, partnerships work whenever all the participants share responsibility and accountability for the work of the partnership. We must be accountable and responsible even if we do not have authority. It can't be us and them; it can only be us. There is no waiting for someone else to act. Authority and accountability are separated. The buck still stops here, but "here" is at every individual's desk, not just the CEO's.

Respect for the Person

Partnership begins with a deep respect for the person; it is based on a deep-down-in-the-gut belief in the inherent worth and value of every person. Partnerships assume that everyone has gifts and skills and energies to offer to the process of cocreation. Partnership honors diversity, in word and deed. It requires that each individual be treated with dignity and respect. Respect for personhood is the sine qua non of partnerships.

This deep belief in the inherent worth of the person includes belief in the worth and value of the self. We shall have trouble honoring and respecting others as long as we think we are of value only if—if we are productive, if we please the boss, if we have the corner office, if we are somehow perfect. Respect for personhood includes respect for our own person.

Partnering in the Nitty-Gritty

Partnership must work in the tough, nitty-gritty aspects of organizational life and leadership practices, as well as in particular and special activities, if it is to work at all. It doesn't strain the imagination to think of people getting together to cocreate a shared vision for their workgroup or organization. Likewise, it seems quite reasonable to assume that individuals might work interdependently to define core values, or develop a mission statement, or cocreate shared goals. But what about individuals working together to make sense out of tough and complex problems? Or about individuals on a self-managed workteam striving together to cocreate a performance appraisal and compensation system that reflects a deeper sense of meaning? Or about two individuals working as partners, rather than as boss and subordinate, to decide if it is time for one to leave his or her present job? (This might be a good time, if you will, to roll the word *subordinate* around on your tongue and see how it really tastes.) In these tough, nitty-gritty situations we usually turn to a boss or manager and want that person to decide, to tell us what to do. But if it is to serve us well, leadership-as-partnership must work in each of these real-world situations.

It is my belief, based on personal experiences and those others have shared with me, that if these five requirements are met, something noticeably new begins to happen in relationships (in partnerships). There is a different feel and tone. There is more vitality and energy. Though not always named, spirit is experienced, elegantly weaving individuals and their relationships.

Partnership in One-to-One Relationships

Martha, Robbie, and Ruth's stories were told at the beginning of Chapter Three. In all three vignettes, the executives-as-leaders acted in ways that were dispiriting. Martha was forced to take an assignment she did not want. Robbie was told to finish a project in a way that he knew would not work. Ruth had a demeaning encounter with an executive-as-leader in her first days on a new and challenging assignment. How would their stories change if their managers understood leadership as something that grows out of the reciprocity of a relationship, if they used a partnership model that fit the requirements I've just outlined?

Let's see how.

Instead of getting a phone call, Martha and her boss sit down face-to-face to engage in dialogue about her gifts, skills, and energies, and where they can best be used to meet the needs of the organization. Instead of dealing with an imposed decision, Martha and her boss agree on one that works for both of them. What's needed is not a boss-centered solution, that is, a solution residing within the boss that probably resolves his needs foremost even if couched in the language of helping the organization. Likewise, and importantly, it also does not work for the boss to accept a Martha-centered solution, one from within her that works for her but not the organization. Instead, they share power and find a relationship-centered solution, a solution from outside of either person that comes instead from the interaction between them. Done in this way, the decision allows Martha to continue her work with renewed enthusiasm and commitment, ready to use her gifts, skills, and energies rather than leave the organization; and the organization retains a valued employee. You'll recall that in the original vignette Martha moved from dependence to counterdependence and finally to independence on her way out of the organization.

You might be thinking, "Sounds good, but it will never work in real life." Or, "Individuals should not expect to get their needs met; the organization writes the check, so the organization decides where an individual is needed." Or, "We are a large organization and it would take too much time to have a career conversation with every employee." The command-and-control, executive-as-leader model appears more efficient, seems more reasonable. In some ways it is. But we don't calculate all the costs. To repeat, whenever coercive power flows one way in a relationship, resentment and hostility flow in the other. Like Martha, if we are treated in a one-down way, if we don't experience deep respect, we not only become dispirited but look for an early exit, literally or figuratively, from the organization.

Robbie, you will remember, knows what he wants from his interaction with his boss. He wants his boss to ask him what he (Robbie) can do to get the project back on schedule rather than being told what to do. Robbie wants dialogue, not direction. He wants partnership, not power over. He wants to be a person, not a puppet. They have a shared goal, so one of the five requirements of partnership is in place. But the boss thinks he knows what needs to be done, he doesn't have a lot of time to discuss it, and he understands his role to be giving direction and making sure priority projects are finished on time. He exercises power over. The boss thinks he is getting what he wants—an obedient employee—however he doesn't really get that at all, because in the original vignette this obedient employee did what he was told and doing what he was told delayed the launch of the new product even more.

Partnerships happen in simple experiences of work. In Robbie's case, a simple hallway conversation killed his spirit and, with it, his enthusiasm for his work. Things could be otherwise. All that is required is for the boss to treat Robbie as a partner in getting a task accomplished that both agree is important, and for Robbie to have sufficient courage to speak his truth to his boss.

Ruth's welcome to a new job was dispiriting for her in the original telling. She was treated in a one-down, demeaning, "make sure you remember that you work for me" way. Already anxious about the challenges she faced in the new job and new culture, she left the first meeting feeling more insecure and uncertain. Her self-confidence was shaken. She decided to avoid interacting with the executive as much as possible, and they both lost in the process. The executive missed out on getting information that would have been helpful to him, and Ruth missed out on opportunities to try to develop an important ally. She also made sure thereafter that she did not intentionally cross him, thus colluding (even if understandably) with some of his worst instincts.

Now imagine the executive inviting Ruth to be a true partner in meeting the needs of the organization, acknowledging that she brings gifts and skills and energies important to the success of the organization, and offering to share his experience and expertise with her to ensure the success of their work together. In this new ending, they cocreate something special rather than the fear and insecurity that was originally created.

I remember the first time I laid off someone who reported to me. It was a gut-wrenching, awful experience. I am still embarrassed about how I did it—in a top-down, command-and-control exercise of coercive power. It was subtle use of coercive power, to be sure, but still very real. Even though there were some questionable aspects to the person's behavior, I didn't fire him; I laid him off. I did away with his job. It sounded better, at least I thought, and it seemed an easier way to do it, because no negatives about the person had to surface. I could simply communicate that we no longer needed his position, which was at least half true. I worked through the decision ahead of time with my boss and the director of human resources. I made sure that the employee was getting what I considered reasonable severance (if I were going to be a dictator, at least I wanted to be benevolent), and I announced the decision to the employee in a meeting of less than ten minutes. I explained the decision very carefully and rationally. I stayed calm. I paid scant attention to any feelings he might have had. A robot could have done it as well. The experience dispirited the employee. It dispirited me. As word leaked out about what had happened, it dispirited others in the organization. It took me days, if not weeks, to feel energized about work that required and deserved all my gifts and energies.

I knew there had to be a better way. The next time I thought a staff member was no longer effective in a position, I decided to handle it differently. We talked. We talked about the needs of the job and the organization, and how her gifts and skills matched those needs. We talked about how the job had changed as our department grew, and we agreed that what once were strengths for her no longer were. We agreed that new skills were now needed if she were to be effective in the role. She asked for an opportunity to develop those skills, and so we put an agreed-upon development plan in place, one that contained specific and measurable behavioral goals and mileposts that would let both of us know how she was measuring up. We talked some more—sometimes tough but always honest conversations about how she was doing, and about how I was doing as a coach and manager. We talked about the pain that the process was causing that we both were feeling. Before the deadline for developing the new skills arrived, she came into my office and acknowledged that her performance wasn't what it needed to be, and she told me she wanted to invest her energies in other pursuits. A colleague whom I had used as a coach during this process said to me when it was over, "This is the way it is supposed to happen. She fired herself." (I tell this story trusting that you will understand that in no way was she fired.)

When she and I started the process, I did not know what the final decision would be. Neither did she. I was determined not to impose a decision on her; I was equally determined to be honest with her, and to make sure I did not accept a decision that simply accommodated her. The decision was cocreated; it evolved from the reciprocity, the give-and-take, that existed in our relationship. We worked as partners to make sense of a difficult situation and decide what would be best for all concerned.

It is quicker and more efficient to make a firing decision using the executive-as-leader model. To use the partnership model takes longer and requires a different skill set. It is just as hard to do the latter, perhaps harder. I know for me the second experience was as gut-wrenching as the first. But the latter acknowledges the importance of the individual, and the former doesn't. One affirms the gifts that individuals bring, even if those gifts no longer fit, and one doesn't. One honors spirit, the other suffocates spirit and drains life from all involved.

Partnership in Teams

For years, Warren Bennis has been one of this country's foremost thinkers and writers on leadership. Much of his work focuses on the traits and characteristics of outstanding individual leaders. Recently, his work has taken him back to the place he started: the importance and power of "great groups." To understand the power of great groups, Bennis and a colleague, Patricia Ward Biederman, studied seven examples: Apple Computer, the Black Mountain Artistic Community, President Clinton's reelection campaign team, Walt Disney's animation studio, the famous "skunk works" of Lockheed, the Manhattan project, and Xerox's PARC (Palo Alto Research Center). One of their conclusions: "In a global society, in which timely information is the most important commodity, collaboration is not simply desirable, it is inevitable. In all but the rarest of cases, one is too small a number to produce greatness" (1997, p. 3).

The emergence and use of workteams—of groups that are great and groups that are not quite so great—may be one of the best indicators that our view and practice of leadership is changing. Not only do workteams contribute to the flattening of organizations but they often operate with much less bureaucracy and with much more innovation and creativity. Workteams can function effectively without a directive leader. Indeed, the success of workteams is dependent on tapping into the mental, physical, emotional, and spiritual energy of their people; committing to these energies comes once each person is made a partner in the process. On effective workteams, leadership happens as people work as partners to accomplish a shared goal.

Leadership-as-partnership works even on those teams and in those situations where one might expect a need for strong, directive leadership by a single person. Studies done of workteams in high-stress situations—cockpit crews, for example—have shown that directive leadership by a single individual is less important than that the team knows how to function together as a close-knit unit. It is the reciprocal relationships in the cockpit that are important; leadership emerges from the interaction of the crew members.

Workteams also experience leadership-as-partnership in their ordinary, day-to-day work. Several years ago, I had the opportunity to work with the executive team of a major consumer products company. Business was good for this operating company, but a young, energetic president knew that the leadership of the organization could be stronger and that the senior team of six people could be more effective. Relationships among the individuals on the team were cordial and harmonious, at least on the surface, but if you scratched the surface you found unresolved conflict and tension. Individual executives had built their fiefdoms, and they worked hard to protect them. They experienced none of the fruits of interdependence; in fact, they avoided it strenuously. Conflicts and disagreements between individual VPs were pushed up to the president for him to resolve. Responsibility and accountability were not shared; instead, if something went wrong in one part of the operation other VPs worked hard to distance themselves from the trouble. There was more finger-pointing and blaming than working toward shared goals. Differences in style and personalities were not honored; there was no appreciation that diversity might be a strength upon which they could build.

All of these characteristics surfaced during the initial round of interviews conducted with the individual executives, the first step in my work with them. During the feedback session with the team, these characteristics were acknowledged, albeit somewhat reluc-tantly and with more than a little defensiveness. It took them time, individually and as a group, to let down their guard and admit that the appearance of harmonious relationships was more fiction than fact. Though hard to hear, data from interviews were a catalyst for change. The data brought to the surface truths about themselves as individuals and as a team that each knew existed but had not pub-licly acknowledged. It provided clear evidence about how their individual and team behaviors were having a negative impact on organizational results.

After the feedback session, two kinds of team-development activities were held, one apart from their regular work as an exec-utive team and one as part of their ongoing work. In these sessions, and in the four months in between, the executives worked on new ways of being and acting together. They worked on acknowledging and holding conflict, on surfacing assumptions, on engaging in real dialogue, on solving problems rather than passing them up to the president, on sharing responsibility for the problems facing the or-ganization. In short, they worked on acting interdependently to cocreate and implement shared goals.

Change did not come quickly; even after they started to change they sometimes reverted to old patterns of interacting. Habits are hard to break. But they did change. As part of my work with them, over the course of the next year I observed and then helped them debrief two of their half-day executive-team meetings. The change in their interactions was clearly noticeable: more open, less guarded; more collaborative, less competitive; more willing to put issues out on the table, less sabotaging after the meeting. They developed new understandings of their role and how they could practice partnership-as-leadership, and over time they developed the capacities needed to act on this new understanding. For this executive team, team development and leadership development were one and the same.

At other times, teams experience partnership-as-leadership on particular and special occasions. Organizations, and the teams within them, are paying particular attention today to developing shared understanding of mission and purpose, of vision and values—those things that give special meaning to work, that answer the *why* question of work. There is a growing realization that a vision, a sense of mission, purpose, and values cannot be imposed, that instead they must all emerge from the interaction of team members. If developing a vision or a mission statement is understood as requiring the use of all of our energies, not just our heads, and if members of the team are treated as true partners in the process, teams experience partnership-as-leadership.

Partnership in Organizations: The Story of Southwest Airlines

The partnership model also works in organizations.

Like American Airlines, Southwest Airlines is a top-five carrier headquartered in Dallas. Over time, Southwest has developed an inspired and enthusiastic workforce, thanks in part to the leadership model it has implemented. To compare and contrast the Southwest story with that of American Airlines (Chapter Three), let me describe the keys to the success of Southwest in some detail.

In Southwest Airlines, leadership is understood as *collaboration* (partnership). Southwest has intentionally changed to a new practice of leadership. Southwest executives realized that the authoritarian style that characterized the first president, Lamar Muse, would not allow them to maintain the esprit de corps they thought critical to the long-term success of the airline. It fostered compliance, not commitment, and Southwest needed the commitment of all its employees if it were to succeed in its tough and demanding business environment. Executives at Southwest learned that the top-down, command-and-control style did not elicit the inspired performance that was needed. "We're trying to apply the typical hierarchical, top-down industrial-society theories to a society that's completely different," Herb Kelleher, chairman, president, and CEO of Southwest is quoted as saying in an interview. "[We need to] take the pyramid and turn it upside down. Turn it on its point. Down here, at the bottom, you've got people at headquarters. Up there, at the top, you've got people who are out in the field on the front lines. They are the ones who make things happen. The people out there are the experts. You can compare our role in the front office to the military: we're the supply corps, we're not the heroes. We supply the heroes, period. The heroes are out there" (Lee, 1994, p. 11).

Today at Southwest, words like *management* and *executive* are seldom used. It is people that are important, regardless of their role, title, or position. "Leadership is practiced through collaborative relationships. The people of Southwest Airlines work in relationships where the role of leader and collaborator are interchangeable" (Freiberg and Freiberg, 1996, p. 299). Every employee has opportunities to participate in the activity of leadership.

"A financial analyst once asked me," Kelleher said, "if I was afraid of losing control of our organization. I told him I've never had control and I never wanted it. If you create an environment where people truly participate, you don't need control. They know what needs to be done, and they do it. And the more people commit themselves to your cause on a voluntary basis, the fewer hierarchies and control mechanisms you need" (Kelleher, 1997, p. 21). People who work in an organization where top-down control is not used have an opportunity to voluntarily commit to their work, to willingly accept responsibility for the shared outcome or goal. In turn, the organization gets commitment rather than compliance.

At Southwest, as in other organizations, there is a relationship between sharing power and control and the commitment of individuals to use all of their energies in the service of their work.

Herb Kelleher is often pictured as larger than life, so much so that it is easy to believe that he is *the* leader and the one person responsible for the growth and profitability of the airline, a perfect example of a successful executive-as-leader. To be sure, he has been and is important. But Southwest has created processes and systems that encourage broad and real participation in the activity of leadership. Leadership in Southwest Airlines grows out of the interdependence and collaboration of people who share a common goal. It evolves from the reciprocity of relationships. Partnerships are more important than any single individual. Kelleher knows this is true. In an interview, he hypothesized: "Now, say someone came into Southwest Airlines and said, 'Herb Kelleher is gone, and I don't subscribe to anything he did. Power is my bag. Hierarchy, bureaucracy—those are the things I love'. I think he'd last about a month. He'd be thrown overboard by the people, because the culture is stronger than any individual" (Lee, 1994, p. 72).

The people of Southwest understand that collaboration and partnership involve new ways of understanding issues of accountability and shared responsibility. All the employees at Southwest are encouraged to be accountable, even in areas for which they don't have authority. Cross training is part of the culture. Pilots learn to work with ramp agents, and customer service agents learn to assist skycaps.

Southwest has a culture that focuses on "*fun*damentals" and honors spirit. The culture of an organization is not easily seen or touched. It is more intangible than tangible. It cannot be quantified. It is more "how things get done around here." It is known through stories that are told, experiences that are celebrated, rituals that preserve important traditions. From programs such as Helping Hands (in which employees from one location volunteer to work weekends in another location) or Walk a Mile in My Shoes (in which Southwest employees were encouraged to spend a day off "walking in the shoes" of a fellow worker; 75 percent of employees did so) to the metaphor of the organization as family, to the first profit-sharing plan in the airline industry, the people of Southwest understand that they are all in this together. At Southwest, the culture creates and sustains partnerships.

From the early days, employees were encouraged to have fun— and they did. From the ways announcements are made on flights to the costumes worn on special occasions, the employees of this self-styled "LUV airline" enjoy their work. Individuality is honored. Humor and creativity find good soil in which to grow. The company does a lot to keep this part of the culture alive, from their "culture committee" of storytellers to videos such as "Southwest Shuffle" (employees rapping about having fun on the job) and "Keepin' the Spirit Alive." There is a relationship between having fun and inspired performance.

The employees have had fun, but they also focus on fundamentals: on-time arrivals, quick turnarounds, low-cost fares, shared responsibility for jobs. This is also part of the culture. They take their *work* seriously, just not themselves. Spirit, personal job performance, and corporate financial performance are linked at Southwest.

And spirit matters there. "We look for people who are unselfish and altruistic and who enjoy life," reports Kelleher. "The focus is on the intangibles, the spiritual qualities, not an individual's educational experience. We can train anybody to do a job, from a technical standpoint. We are looking for people with an esprit de corps, an attitude" (Verespej, 1995, p. 22). At Southwest, no one has to leave spirit at home or locked safely in the trunk of the car out in the company parking lot. As a result, the people of Southwest offer inspired, innovative performance to the organization.

The force called spirit is a competitive advantage for Southwest. "In an industry where every carrier has access to the same kind of equipment, Southwest's real competitive advantage is the spiritual energy used by its people . . . it [isn't] surprising to see that the overwhelming majority of articles in the business press focus on the operations of Southwest Airlines, not on the spirit of its people. Perhaps this is because spirit is hard to define; operational techniques are much more tangible and therefore easier to learn and replicate" (Freiberg and Freiberg, 1996, p. 327). At Southwest, leadership and spirit are closely linked.

But what about the bottom line? Can an organization that acknowledges the importance of spirit, that focuses on partnership and the *fun* in fundamentals, and that is consistently rated as one of the best places to work in the United States be profitable? The answer from Southwest is an unqualified yes. The company has enjoyed twenty-five years of consistent profitability and was the only major airline to make net and operating profits in the years 1990 to 1992. From modest and uncertain beginnings in 1971, Southwest has grown to become the fifth largest domestic airline, in terms of domestic passengers served.

The Airlines Compared: American and Southwest

A comparison of the two companies is telling.

In some ways they look similar. Both companies are leaders in the airline industry. Both have been financially successful. Both are credited with introducing changes that profoundly affected the airline industry. Among other instances, at a time when other carriers were using a hub-and-spoke system, Southwest introduced a low-fare, high-frequency, point-to-point system; for its part, American is credited with starting frequent-flyer award programs and introducing the Sabre system. Both have well-known executives at the helm (though as this was being written, Crandall announced his retirement from American).

But then the stories begin to diverge. Crandall fit prototypically the model of a command-and-control leader. He threatened, he bullied, he cajoled, he coerced. He publicly humiliated American pilots. During his watch, there was no sharing of power, responsibility, and accountability, no deep respect for the person. During his tenure, American was successful, but it was not a fun place to work.

In many ways, some large and some small and subtle, the organization suffocated spirit.

Southwest has a different leadership model and a different culture. As pointed out earlier, the people of Southwest have fun while taking care of the fundamentals. Power and responsibility are shared. Kelleher does not even want to control his people; he knows that commitment works better than compliance. Partnership is apparent in how decisions are made and responsibility is shared. The organization, and the people in it, pay attention to spirit. They know it matters.

Here's the point, and it is an important one: it is possible to be successful, even highly successful, and have a dispirited workforce. But it doesn't have to be that way. As Southwest and countless other companies have shown, organizations can nurture and heed that unseen force called spirit *and* be profitable. I suggest that's why Southwest was recently named number one on *Fortune* magazine's list of the 100 best companies to work for in America (Levering and Moskowitz, 1998, p. 84).

The Partnership Model in Other Organizations

Other organizations are implementing a version of the partnership model. Let me mention but a few of them.

• W. L. Gore has no bosses, little bureaucracy, and no titles (individuals can select the title they want on their business cards). It has employees who are associates. The culture precludes the use of direct orders, and the company fosters collaboration and partnerships by organizing itself and its facilities so that no more than two hundred people work in one place. The result: W. L. Gore has energized employees known for developing innovative products, with Gore-Tex (the product that keeps us dry on wet days) being the best known example. Leadership is a distributed process in this organization.

• Skaltek is a Swedish company that produces cable-and-wire-handling machines. They use peer communities to organize and do their work. No external control systems are imposed on these communities. Rather than leading to anarchy as some might fear, this approach has led instead to a flexible and responsive company.

• Herman S. Miller has gained wide recognition for innovative furniture design. It is a company with some enduring principles: the importance of covenantal relationships (relationship based on shared commitment rather than fear), a core belief that the company must have a redemptive purpose and help people reach their potential as well as meet company goals, conviction that executives must be willing to "abandon themselves to the strengths of others," and recognition of the importance of spirit.

• Human Service Alliance (HSA) is a nonprofit organization located in Winston-Salem, North Carolina, that operates with one of the purest partnership models I have found. HSA offers four services. The Center for the Terminally Ill provides around-the-clock care to guests whose life expectancy is less than six months. The Respite Care Projects offer families who have a child with a developmental disability a temporary rest. The Health and Wellness Project provides holistic health care. The Mediation Project assists individuals in resolving conflicts in a win-win way. HSA serves men and women from all segments of society. Some are poor, others are wealthy; but the truth is the quality of service provided by the all-volunteer staff could not be bought at any price. AT HSA, spirit is made visible in the quality of its care. HSA has no executive. It has no hierarchy, not even a turned-upside-down hierarchy. Instead, leadership in this organization happens in the partnerships created and used by volunteers as they work collaboratively to accomplish deeply held and shared goals.

Objections to the Partnership Model

Significant questions are often raised about leadership-as-partnership. Without assuming that I know or can adequately answer all objections or questions, I want to address the issues most often raised.

"It Diminishes the Role of the Individual"

The objection I hear most often to the idea of partnership-as-leadership is that it diminishes the role of the individual. I think the contrary is true. In this model, the role of the individual is enhanced even as it is put in a new context.

Although leadership is not the province of a single individual in the partnership model, the personhood of each individual involved becomes more important. The gifts, skills, and energies of each person in the relationship are honored and put to use. Individual uniqueness is honored, authenticity is valued, and differences are acknowledged and held, not brushed aside or quickly solved. There is no "more than" or "less than"—more important than, less important than; more powerful than, less powerful than; more gifted than, less gifted than. There is no one-up or one-down, no person having power over and others feeling powerless. Leadership is cocreated by people sharing power.

Furthermore, it is often an individual who is the catalyst for starting the leadership process, of suggesting new ways of working and being together. It can be the refreshing perspective of a person who suggests new ways of finding meaning and purpose in work. Or a single individual walking the talk—living out important values—and freeing others to do likewise.

Growing out of the interaction of people working interdependently, roles for individuals are defined; one becomes the spokesperson, another is the organizer, and yet another one assumes responsibility for the processes that keep the partnership strong and growing. Not all have the gifts, the skills, or the energy to be the spokesperson. But they have other gifts important to the process of partnering. A spokesperson who emerges as a result of the interaction of members of the community or workgroup is more likely to understand his or her role as steward or servant of the community rather than as its master.

Individuals are important in this different model of leadership. But to be honest, the model does suggest a change in perspective.

It suggests that we need to move to more interdependent ways of thinking and acting. The rugged individuals we have held up as our heroic leaders have a hard time acknowledging that they need others, and a hard time acting interdependently. But none of us can be totally independent or totally self-sufficient. We cannot even be our true selves, cannot be the unique individuals we were created to be, unless we acknowledge our need for connectedness to others and share common experiences with them.

In authentic partnerships and communities, individuals flourish. But the importance of relationships and community is also acknowledged and honored. Saying that leadership is an activity that happens in a partnership does not diminish the importance of the individual, but it does suggest that meaning comes from within individuals and from relationships.

"We Need a Great Leader"

Throughout history, some argue, it is the great individual leader who has gotten things done and who is remembered. We think of leadership and remember leaders: along with the figures mentioned in Chapter Three, think of political leader Susan B. Anthony; leaders of social movements such as Martin Luther King Jr., Mahatma Gandhi, and Clara Barton; and such contemporary business leaders as Jack Welch and Mary Kay Ash. They were or are strong, dominant men and women. We make heroes out of them.

The partnership model seems to negate the importance of heroic figures, or so we think. But consider these ideas:

It enhances the importance of all. The partnership model doesn't set out to diminish the role of given individuals. As I've mentioned, the partnership model is based on the assumption that all individuals have gifts, skills, and energies to offer to the activity of leadership and, at various points in an individual's career and life these gifts, skills, and energies are needed in the activity of leadership. Because men and women who come together in partnership bring their own gifts to the activity of leadership these gifts are, of necessity, used differently. Some emerge as individual "leaders." But a leader who emerges from the reciprocal relationship of people in partnership is and acts differently than does a person in that role who is appointed to the position.

It obliges us to question uncritical assumptions about the executive-as-leader. Even as we think of great individual leaders and the impact they've had, there is a question as to whether the leader is as important as we have assumed him or her to be. As Collins and Porras suggest, "perhaps the continuity of superb individuals atop visionary companies stems from the companies being superb organizations, not the other way around" (1994, p. 34). The example they use is Jack Welch of General Electric. Collins and Porras give Welch credit for having "immense energy" and for having a "huge role in revitalizing GE," but they also argue that Welch was "a product of GE as much as the other way around." Welch has been and is important in the company, but through the years GE has developed and put into place systems and processes that find, support, and develop men and women like him. The culture of the organization, and the norms and processes that are embedded in it, create the leader more than the leader creates the culture.

One leader can only do so much. There is a limit, especially these days, to what any individual can do. First, with the increasing diversity of the workforce, it is more and more difficult, if not impossible, for any individual to create and articulate a common vision, one that elicits commitment from most of the men and women of the organization. This may have been possible when the workforce was more homogeneous, but a single-minded workforce is part of a bygone era. As the world changes, our understanding and practice of leadership must also change. Today, a shared vision is possible only if the diverse interests and different agendas of many stakeholders are combined. Shared visions emerge from the reciprocal relationships of people; they cannot be imposed on them. Second, the resources—the gifts, skills, and energies of a single person—invariably run out. It is dangerous to allow one person to occupy center stage too much of the time or to play the sole leading role. To be successful over the long haul, companies need systems, structures, and practices of leadership that call forth the energies of all employees. Finally, the very idea of executive-as-leader does not have built into it what's needed if organizations are going to be innovative enterprises capable of making the constant changes necessary in these turbulent times. This is not an indictment of the men and women in these roles; the problem is with how we have defined the role.

"Partnership Is Naïve About Power"

The partnership model, it is claimed, is based on a naïve view of power. Too many times to count, I have heard the lament from the people with whom I have been privileged to work—from frontline supervisors to senior-level executives—that they need more power, not less, and the power they need, they think, is the power to control. To them, the idea of leadership-as-partnership (an idea that turns the notion of power on its side) seems quaint, even wrongheaded. But before you agree with them, read on.

As suggested in Chapter Three, in the executive-as-leader model, executives often have the power to coerce people into doing what they don't want to do, don't always need to do, or even ought to do (I said earlier that being obedient to a flawed command is one way people have of fighting back). As long as the leader has something the followers want or fear losing, and the followers are either dependent on the leader for the reward or else fear the punishment, the leader can use coercive power.

Years ago, when I was beginning to do management-development work in business and industry, one of my first clients was a large manufacturing company located in the Midwest. I did the work in collaboration with internal organization development consultants. The intervention was started because the business environment of the company had recently changed, forcing it to rely less on defense-related contracts and more on commercial business. There was a shared agreement, especially at the top levels of the organization, that the company was going to have to improve productivity, reduce turnover, create more cooperation among functional areas that were operating from a turf mentality, and get more widespread participation from all workers if it were going to effectively compete in the new environment.

We started our intervention with an organizational survey and learned, among other things, that too much of the communication only flowed from the top down, that decisions were pushed up, that relationships were characterized by fear and mistrust (the paper trail in this company was a long one; the most commonly used management techniques was CYA), that too many bosses operated with the my-way-or-the-highway mentality (this is where I was introduced to this phrase—I heard it a lot in this company). In the parlance of this book, employees were a dispirited lot.

The threat of the highway worked in this company because employees feared it. Economic times were tough in those days, and jobs—especially high-paying hourly jobs—were scarce. Command-and-control tactics work more effectively when times are tough, because we fear the highway and more quickly give away our power, more willingly allow bosses to be coercive. But it is too easy to say that the answer at this company, or any other, is for employees to simply refuse to be coerced. For real change to happen, bosses and employees alike have to adopt a different understanding and practice of leadership. This is the kind of change the company decided to embrace and implement. Long before cross-functional, self-managed workteams were popular, the company began its movement in that direction. Before the concept of empowerment became a fad, the company took clear, slow steps to implement a version of it.

Many managers in the company welcomed the new initiatives, became advocates of them, and worked hard to develop the skills they needed to be successful in this new environment. Others did not. They had grown comfortable with the old ways of managing, and they liked exercising their coercive power. They thought that my way or the highway was the only approach that ensured that workers would pay attention and be productive. They were rugged individualists, or so they thought. The complaint most often heard from these supposed individualists was that as the company took away the carrot and stick—their ability to coerce—it took away their power.

This is a lament I have heard often through the years. I have heard it from parents, teachers, school administrators, supervisors, and executives. The underlying assumption is that the only power people have is the power to reward or punish. Take away the carrot and stick, and you render individuals powerless. This is based on the belief that the only real source of power is the power to coerce.

What those in the management roles—parents, teachers, and executives alike—have failed to realize is that a stick and a carrot are not the sources of real power. Coercive power held by executives-as-leaders is only on loan from followers, and followers can call the note on a moment's notice. Managers and executives can use coercive power only if followers let them. For those who need to coerce to feel powerful, the hard truth is that it is followers who decide if the manager has power. Chester Barnard, at one time the president of New Jersey Bell Telephone, told us, way back in 1938, that "the decision as to whether or not an order has authority or not lies with the person to whom it is addressed." But we have a hard time accepting that this is true. (I learned this truth as a parent when I told one of my daughters, then about six, that she couldn't have dessert unless she finished all the food on her plate. She let me know, as only a six-year-old can, that she didn't want dessert anyway. She was not about to be coerced.)

In partnerships, power has a different source. It comes from within the person. Its source is the gifts, skills, and energies that belong to the person. It is personal rather than coercive. We claim our personal power as we own our gifts and skills, our competence and our expertise, and begin to use them with confidence in the relationships of which we are a part. We claim our personal power as we learn to embrace our fears and dependencies, including our fear of losing a job and our dependency on a benevolent dictator, because as we embrace our fears they lose some of their grip on us. We claim our personal power as we embrace our shadow, as we begin to own it as a part of ourselves. We claim our personal power as we accept the opportunity and responsibility to be cocreators. We claim our personal power as we learn to use all of our energies (mental, physical, emotional, and spiritual) in our work.

Each of us has personal power; not all of us use it. In the *Four-Fold Way*, Angeles Arrien says, "Many indigenous societies believe that we all possess 'original medicine': personal power duplicated nowhere else on the planet. No two individuals carry the same combination of talents and challenges" (1993, p. 21). Our task is to appreciate, lay claim to, and begin to use our original medicine.

Power is still present in the relationship, but it comes from within the individuals, not from a position. No person has power over others. The partnership model is based on covenant and not coercion, on commitment and not compliance. It may sound quaint, but in the long run personal power is the only source of real power we have.

We must change our basic assumption about power if we are to claim and use it effectively. As long as we believe that power is a limited resource, our tendency is to hoard it. We protect our turf, we do not share information or knowledge, and we try to make sure we have more than others. But if, by contrast, we assume that power is not a limited resource, that it is available to all people and is fed by all four of our energies, then our understanding of power, and our relationship to it, is changed.

Though it sounds similar, the partnership model is not another name for empowerment. Empowerment suggests that one person— the leader—shares her power with others—the followers. It is based on an assumption that power is a currency one person can give or share with another. Phrases we use and hear such as "I empowered them" or "They gave us the power to decide" suggest the perspective behind the empowerment.

The partnership model is based on the assumption that power cannot be given, but only claimed. It is claimed as we understand our gifts and skills, as we act on our competence and expertise, as we are courageous. It comes from deep within us and is claimed, not given to us. The partnership model assumes that all of us are powerful, that we must each claim our power for collective leadership to emerge and spirit to surface.

"It's Not Forceful Enough"

Partnership-as-leadership lacks forcefulness and urgency. We tend to believe, it seems to me, that an organization's success is dependent on having a forceful, aggressive executive-as-leader driving the troops hard to get maximum results. Partnerships just cannot have the same sense of urgency, or so we think.

This point was brought home to me in work I did recently with the management team of Midwestern commodities business. Midway through a team-development process, the president, in her clear and to-the-point way, told me in a private conversation that we were not yet addressing the core issue she wanted on the table. She explained: her predecessor had been a hands-on micromanager. He got involved in the details—too involved. He did not share responsibility and accountability. He wanted decisions pushed up. The new president was determined to be different. She wanted all VPs to claim their power. She wanted them to share responsibility and accountability. She did not want them pushing decisions up, or waiting to find out what she wanted before acting. The president was determined that they would accomplish the goals they had all agreed to, and she wanted it to be done through a process of shared leadership. She feared, though, that the VPs were so used to a top-down leadership style, and that they so lacked her sense of urgency, that they were neither prepared nor willing to step up to the plate and be accountable. We agreed that the next morning the president would express her fear to the group.

She did. She told the group things she knew about herself, how competitive she was, how much she hated to lose. She talked about her sense of urgency, and how it led at times to in-your-face interactions. She told them that she feared that they did not share her competitiveness or her sense of urgency. None of what she said surprised any of the VPs; they all knew it and had talked about it in one-to-one conversations. But they had never talked about it in a team setting. After a moment of silence, one of the quietest and most soft-spoken of the VPs said to the president: "We are just as competitive as you and feel the same sense of urgency as you. We feel just as accountable as you. We obviously don't show it in the same way, but it is there." A deeply helpful conversation ensued.

Partnerships can share a deep sense of urgency and act forcefully to accomplish agreed-upon goals. These were some of the characteristics of the great groups mentioned earlier. Urgency and forcefulness are not attributes held only by individuals.

"It Destroys Accountability"

People fear that partnership-as-leadership diminishes individual accountability. If all are accountable, the skeptic suggests, no one is. The buck must stop somewhere; a team cannot really be accountable.

Historically, individual accountability has been part and parcel of management and executive roles. As hierarchies are created, accountability is built in, the level of accountability corresponding to the level in the organization, with the buck finally stopping at the CEO's door. Accountability and authority are linked. We cannot (we have long argued) be accountable unless we have authority, and this authority is given to us by someone else. Along with accountabilities, individuals get the authority needed to meet them. Then, in this model, systems are put in place to assess how well the accountabilities are met, and compensation systems are created to reward those who accomplish the work for which they are accountable.

The system works, or so it seems, in top-down, command-and-control organizations, ones in which *leader* and *executive* are still used interchangeably. But it works only if control is more important than commitment and compliance more important than creativity, and if the leader-as-executive is willing to have legions of followers who feel no responsibility or accountability for the outcomes. If accountability is structured into management levels in hierarchical organizations, decisions get pushed up and orders get sent down. If accountability belongs only to those in positions of authority, they are responsible and we are not. The organization can no longer afford for the few to be accountable for the many.

Partnerships require that all the people in the relationship, workgroup, organization, or community become more responsible and accountable for what happens. Now, we are they. We must forgo the notion that it is the role of the leader to be fully accountable. We must no longer believe that real change in any organization can only start at the top. We must accept responsibility for ourselves, for the relationships and partnerships to which we belong, and for the work of the organization. We must understand and act on our role as cocreator. To make this new understanding and practice of leadership a reality, we must accept responsibility and accountability for the workgroup even if we don't have the authority we have long thought we needed.

In *Stewardship*, Peter Block makes this point: "Each person [in a partnership] is responsible for outcomes and the current situation. There is no one else to blame. Partners have emotional responsibility for their own present and their own future . . . the outcomes and quality of cooperation within a unit are everyone's responsibility. Each is responsible for maintaining faith, hope, and spirit. . . . The central point is that if people want the freedom that partnership offers, the price of that freedom is to take personal responsibility for the success and failure of our unit and our community" (1993, p. 30).

For partnership to work, ownership, authority, and accountability must be felt at every level, by every person.

The Two Models: A Contrast

Point-by-point summaries usually leave too much unsaid. But they also can provide a useful snapshot of key ideas. So here, offered with some hesitation, is a comparison and contrast of the executive-as-leader and partnership models of leadership.

Executive-as-Leader	Partnership
Leadership comes from an individual	Leadership results from the interaction within a relationship
The buck stops at the top	Shared accountability
Basis of power is coercive	Basis of power is positional and personal
Individual is important	Individual and community are important
Results in efficiency and control	Results in creativity and inspired performance
Spirit is ignored or, worse, suffocated	Attention is paid to spirit

Partnership and Spirit

In partnerships, spirit matters. It is recognized as important, not as something peripheral to the business—or worse, something that has no place in business. Spirit matters not because it is seen as just another tactic to get people to do more with less, or as a source of competitive advantage, though perhaps it is; rather, it matters because people matter.

In partnership relationships, the gifts, skills, and energies of all the people are used. Differences are honored. Dialogue replaces diatribe. Conflict is held, or resolved in a win-win way, rather than being ignored or resolved in a win-lose way. Power, responsibility, and accountability are shared. Courage replaces collusion, commitment replaces compliance, and employees offer inspired performance rather than doing just enough to get by. Leadership is understood as true partnership. Because these things happen, spirit is more likely to be experienced at every level of the organization and in all relationships.

There is a link between how leadership is practiced and how (or whether) we experience the presence of spirit.

In the next part, we turn our attention to who all of us must be, and what all of us must do, if we are to move toward a new way of working and leading together—if we are to make explicit the link between leadership and spirit.

Part Two

Ways of Being, Ways of Doing

Chapter Five

Who Are We to Be?

> So the point is not to become a leader. The point is
> to become yourself, to use yourself completely—all
> your skills, gifts, and energies—in order to make your
> vision manifest. You must withhold nothing. You
> must, in sum, become the person you started out to
> be, and enjoy the process of becoming.
> —*Warren Bennis (1989, pp. 111–112)*

Personal development, including the weaving together of the threads of leadership and spirit, is an ongoing, lifelong journey. We don't change quickly; our ways of being and our patterns of behavior are hard to break. But most of us do learn and grow and change over the course of our lives. With time, and from lots of experiences, we redefine and recreate ourselves and develop and integrate new leadership skills and capacities. We are not the same persons we were ten years ago, and we will again be changed ten years from now.

On Personal Development

This affirmative view of change is important because all of us must change if we are to move toward a partnership model. Command-and-control leaders must learn new ways of being leaders and doing leadership; those of us who have been called followers must also learn new ways of being in relationships and participating in the activity of leadership.

Like other developmental experiences, some of the change and growth we undergo on this journey toward partnership-as-leadership is naturally occurring. We have experiences and we learn from them, especially from those that challenge us and push us out of our comfort zone. In the midst of these experiences we are not always aware of changing; the awareness comes with retrospection. We look back and realize we are today somehow not who we were before, and that our understanding and practice of leadership is also not what it was. We did not plan on changing, or decide to change, or work on changing. Rather, we had the experiences, and we learned from them.

But some change and growth requires intent, our decision to be and do differently. Not all change and growth occurs naturally. Learning is not always automatic; it does not always happen with the ebb and flow of life. Because this is true, some developmental experiences have to be planned and structured, and learning has to be assisted by support and feedback from others.

To be sure, not all individuals are willing or able to change. Some individuals are blocked learners. There are executives-as-leaders, individuals in important positions of power and authority, who either cannot or will not change. Their mantra is "you can't teach an old dog new tricks." The assumption behind the chant is that executives get to a point in their lives or careers where they cannot learn. It seems more likely that they choose not to. Command-and-control leaders who are comfortable with their practice of leadership, who fervently believe that it is the way to get best results, who isolate themselves from feedback about the impact of the leadership style, and who live solely in the external world and never consider an inner journey of discovery are choosing not to learn and grow. There are also followers who are blocked learners, who choose not to grow. They are comfortable being dependent on a leader and don't want the accountability or responsibility that comes with being included in the activity of leadership. They are also stuck in a particular way of being and doing.

But most individuals, as many as 70 percent of workers (Bunker and Webb, 1992), are able and willing to learn, grow, and change. Learners look for experiences that challenge them. They are open to feedback that confirms or confronts their way of being and doing, and they get support from organizations and individuals as they work to develop the new capacities that enable them to function effectively in the leadership processes.

The development journey toward actualizing partnership-as-leadership is similar to other developmental journeys in many ways, but in one significant way it is not: this journey, which includes paying attention to spirit and implementing practices of leadership that honor it, is as much about our being as our doing, as much about inner life as external relationship. It is to these dimensions of development that we now turn our attention.

The Important Assumption: The Focus Must Be on Being and Doing

We know *what* leaders are supposed to do. We've studied it, written about it, taught it. In the executive-as-leader model, the one we have studied and taught the most, leaders are to create and articulate a vision, develop strategies, implement ways of organizing work to make sure the strategies are accomplished, allocate resources, make decisions, and ensure a fair return to stockholders.

We have also studied and taught *how* leaders are supposed to do the *what*: how to plan and organize, how to influence, how to negotiate, how to empower, how to listen, how to reward and recognize others. In short, we know *how* to get the *what* done efficiently and effectively.

But we have paid scant attention to the *who* that is doing the *what* and the *how*. By and large, our research, writing, and teaching haven't focused on understanding and nurturing the self who is engaged in leadership. It is my conviction that in the activity of leadership the *who* is more important than the *what* or the *how*.

Our current business ethos is tilted toward doing: getting the job done, making the numbers, satisfying the customers, making sure stockholders get a good return on their investment. We are human doers more than human beings. We spend a lot of time in "pure doing" before we recognize the emptiness of it. It is only when our singular focus on doing leads us to personal and spiritual bankruptcy that we begin to question it. Because of our focus on doing, we wind up leading double lives, suffering from what consultant and author Richard Leider called "legitimized schizophrenia": we know, at some deep level that there is a disconnect between who we are and what we do, that we are not what we do, but we continue our focus—at times, a frenzied focus—on doing.

As long as we continue this focus on doing and, related to it, continue to develop new leadership skills and behaviors to help us do more effectively, without a corresponding focus on understanding the self who is involved in leadership activities, we can use our expanded skill set as well as models and techniques we learn to more effectively hide the self and falsely portray it to others. We gain facility in wearing a mask and playing the game. We legitimize our schizophrenia. We experience spiritual dis-ease.

The bottom line of this chapter is this: we must know ourselves and be our true and whole selves if we are to successfully and effectively engage in the activity of leadership. Being and becoming ourselves is important to our participation in partnerships. We must bring more balance to our lives; we must focus on being and doing. This chapter and the next describe ways we can move toward this balance.

The questions we must answer as we seek this balance include: What deep longings and aspirations—parts of our best selves—stay hidden deep within, because we don't think our work or the activities of leadership in which we have been engaged are worthy of them? What mental, physical, emotional, and spiritual energy has been lying dormant and is now being rebirthed? Who is the self lurking in the shadow, and how does this part of the self have an impact on our engagement in leadership activities? Who is the whole self beyond the shadow, and can we use our whole self in the activity of leadership?

The answers to these questions are important because, as Bennis reminds us in the quotation opening this chapter, the point is not to become a leader. The point is to become who we started out to be. The adult task is to become ourselves, but too often we refuse this task and settle for something less. It is possible to be ourselves in the framework of work and in leadership activities, but too often we settle for being a caricature.

The Difficulty of Knowing Our Self

Even if we decide to focus on being as well as doing, it is not easy to know and be our true selves. Answers to *who am I?* are more complex than simple, more obscure than obvious, more changing than static. Answering these questions is at the heart of the spiritual journey. It is a difficult journey. Jung argues that there can be no birth of consciousness, no new discoveries about the self, without some pain. We often move from one level of consciousness about ourselves to another in response to challenges—hardships, mistakes, failures, traumas—that demonstrate to us that our present understandings of self are inadequate.

One reason that knowing the self is difficult is that many of us spend at least part of our lives being who someone else wanted us to be. We try to live up (or down) to others' expectations, hiding our true selves under layers of messages from well-meaning adults about who we ought to be or how we ought fulfill their view of our destiny. Charles Handy is a well-known business writer, a former executive with Shell Oil; he was one of the first faculty members of the London Business School. In his latest book, *The Hungry Spirit* (1998), he describes how early in his life he masked his real self:

> I spent the early part of my life trying hard to be someone else. At
> school I wanted to be a great athlete, at university an admired
> socialite, afterwards a businessman and, later, the head of a great

institution. It did not take me long to discover that I was not destined to be successful in any of these guises, but that did not prevent me from trying, and being perpetually disappointed with myself. The problem was that in trying to be someone else I neglected to concentrate on the person I could be. The idea was too frightening to contemplate at the time. I was happier going with the conventions of the time, measuring success in terms of money and position, climbing ladders that others placed in my way, collecting things and contacts rather than giving expression to my own beliefs and personality. I was, in retrospect, hiding from myself, a slave to the system rather than its master [p. 79].

My own story is similar. I remember early in life trying to be the person my parents wanted me to be. My father wanted in the worst way for me to be a scout and to achieve the Eagle rank in scouting; I wanted to be a baseball player, the Chip Hilton of my community. I invested a lot of time and energy in scouting, sometimes missing ball games to do it; but as important as scouting was to many of my friends, it wasn't me. It wasn't what I wanted to do; it wasn't who I wanted to be. My father was a successful executive, an accountant by education and experience, and so years later as I entered college he encouraged me to study business. It was practical. It would lead to a good job. I finally took an accounting course, not because I wanted to or because I thought that it fit any native talent I had, but because it would please Dad. It was an unhappy experience. It was his definition of a good career, not mine. It was the place where he was gifted, not I. But still I tried to meet his expectations.

In more recent years, I have had a similar experience, this time trying to meet the expectation of a boss on how to be and what to do in the workplace. Several years ago, I told the boss to whom I reported that I was ready for a change, that I was no longer energized by the work I was doing and wanted to use my gifts in a new way. He suggested that I would not be happy "playing on a smaller stage" and persuaded me that the organization needed me to stay in my present role. I continued in that role and did the best I could, but I did not have all of myself to give to it. The problems that at one time were challenging were now frustrating. The tasks that once gave me energy now left me feeling drained. More often than not, I left work feeling used up. Trying to meet the expectations of others, no matter how well meaning they are, is climbing someone else's ladder, singing someone else's song, rather than our own. It is dispiriting.

(The rest of the story? I later went to a new boss to engage him in a conversation about my need to use my energies in some other way. This time the result was different. We cocreated a work assignment that fit with my sense of "calling" and that met the needs of the organization. This experience was, for me, an example of partnership-as-leadership in action).

Another reason that the journey to self is not easy is that the self continues to evolve. We are not the same person we were ten years ago. We will be another person tomorrow.

Psychologist Carl Rogers described one way we grow as our "actualizing tendency." He argued that you and I evolve because of "the directional trend which is evident in all organic and human life—the urge to expand, extend, mature—the tendency to express and activate all the capacities of the organization, or the self" (1961, p. 351). For Rogers, our growth is toward autonomy and away from control by external forces. It is growth toward becoming a person or becoming ourselves.

Robert Kegan (1982) has written about the evolving self. In a book by that name, he argues that each of us goes through stages of development; that each stage is distinct, with later stages building on earlier ones; and that each of us tends to go through the stages in the same order. Whereas Rogers believed that our movement or growth is toward autonomy or independence, Kegan's model suggests that as we evolve we move toward independence *and* integration. It is a both-and model.

Perhaps the best-known theory of stage development in management and leadership circles is the one developed by Maslow, popularly known as his hierarchy of needs. We start, he suggested, with a concern with meeting our needs for survival—our need for food, air, and water—and progress toward the final stage, self-actualization. We have used and taught this model in many management and leadership development programs to foster a better understanding of one way in which individuals differ: they are at various places in the hierarchy of needs.

The truth underlying all three of these models, and others similar to them, is that we do grow, change, evolve. We are as much process as static entity; we are being and becoming. To say "I know myself" is to say that I know me at a particular point and time, and at a particular stage of my development.

So the journey to self is neither easy nor quick. Because we evolve and change, the journey lasts our whole life. Some seem unwilling to do the hard and deep work necessary to complete this journey; others start but turn back before the journey is complete. But those who stay the course become the person they started out to be. They find their own voice, their own truth. Along the path they not only understand their true self but also claim their gifts, heed their call, move toward wholeness, and learn to be authentic.

Understanding the Forces That Shape Us

Understanding our self also requires that we understand the interplay of the forces that shape us. The question is as profound as it is simple: What are the forces that have shaped us, and are shaping us? How much knowledge do we have of those forces?

In recent years, we have learned self-awareness is an important attribute of those who engage in the activities of leadership. Our identity helps determine how we understand and practice leadership and engage in relationships that are integral to it. Individuals engaged in the practice of leadership must know their strengths and weaknesses, their personality preferences, what drives and motivates them, and how they have an impact on others. Feedback of various sorts, psychometric instruments, personality preference questionnaires, assessment centers, psychological interviews, IQ tests, and work and interest inventories are just some of the ways we have put individuals under the microscope to help them enhance their awareness of themselves, and learn how they have an impact on others.

But understanding the forces that shape us is more than combining IQ with a collection of behaviors, seasoned by a dose of personality. It is much more complex than that. Identity is more than what we can learn about ourselves from the behavioral sciences, as helpful as they are. There are forces shaping us that are beyond the scope of the behavioral sciences. To think that we can know all there is to know about ourselves from one or more of the behavioral sciences is to fall into the trap of thinking that empiricism and rationalism have all the answers. As Vaill reminds us, "the facts—and the methods of American behavioral science—deal only with commonness. What about specialness?" (1998, p. 26). It is the particular combination of these other forces that creates our specialness.

Chuck Palus, a colleague, suggests that identity is the point on the intersection where all the forces that shape us come together. Sometimes we locate ourselves at a physical spot on the intersection: "I'm a Texan," "I'm a native," "I'm from Japan." At other times we identify ourselves by our memberships in a political party, a religious denomination, a fraternal order. We also locate ourselves at the intersection by jobs or titles, by career choices, by such personal roles as father or wife, or even by sexual preference.

Some of the forces that meet at that intersection are internal to us—our genetic makeup, our native gifts, our shadow—and we locate ourselves on the intersection because of our recognition of these forces. Other forces are external to us; they include the country and culture in which we live, and even the impact that the organization in which we work has on us.

I think about the external forces that have shaped me. I am a white, Anglo-Saxon, Protestant American. Being a WASP is part of my identity. I spent my childhood in the South, and so Southern culture is one of the forces defining me, for good or bad. My family was rather typical: two parents who were married for more than fifty years; and two sisters, one older, one younger. Today I often see one or the other of my parents in me, as part of what I do, but more important, as part of who I am. There has been enough work done on birth order in recent years that I am convinced that being the middle child was also a molding force. There were other adults during the early years who nurtured me, and some who caused me pain; both influenced who I am today. I was a young adult during the 1960s, which encompassed the Vietnam war years, and this experience had an impact on me. Today my identity is still being shaped, by those with and for whom I work, by those I love and who love me, and by those with whom I have a troubled relationship, for whatever the reason. My identity has been, and is being, shaped by external forces.

Another external force that has shaped me, and you of course, has been the organizations for which we have worked and to which we have belonged. Mind you, organizations cannot determine our identity. But they are a force that shapes us, one of the forces that we find at the intersection. We can become more aware of our self by understanding how we internalize aspects of the groups to which we belong.

In some organizations, we are pulled away from asking questions of our specialness and uniqueness by the perceived need to be who the organization expects us to be. In others, and especially those in which some form of partnership-as-leadership is practiced, our specialness is honored.

Another part of identity is shaped by internal forces. Internal drive and ambition, our energy level, the shadow we carry, and our genetic makeup are some of the forces at the intersection. There are those who argue that our genetic makeup is one of the forces that not only shapes us but in fact *determines* us. Forget the shaping of early childhood experiences. Forget the impact of formal educational experiences. Forget the possibility of identity being forged on the anvil of hardship. Forget even the possibility that we can develop. Identity is determined, the argument goes, at the moment of conception.

The problem with this view, of course, is that it takes freedom and responsibility away from the person. External and internal forces have their impact, they shape and mold us, sometimes in ways we do not recognize. But life is not determined by these forces. We have choices and we can, within limits, recreate ourselves. Identity is not a static reality; it can be, and is, a changing reality. Like other aspects of the self, it can and does evolve.

Beyond our genetic makeup, other forces that are internal to us help shape us. One of them is the unseen life force called spirit. It is spirit that weaves through us and gives us, at least in part, our specialness. Understanding spirit is the core to understanding ourselves.

Our shadow is another internal force that shapes our identity. We carry it with us. Our fears, our insecurities, our unresolved guilt and anger, and our dependency needs that we try to keep covered are also at that intersection where identity is known. That which lies unexamined deep within us, the part of us that remains hidden from ourselves as well as others, is part of our identity.

Getting to know the unexamined part of our inner lives is an important aspect of getting to know the self that is engaged in the activity of leadership. In Chapter Three, I described how several executives fostered disconnection out of their unexamined shadow. They are not alone. All of us project shadow onto others and foster disconnection, to a greater or lesser degree. Our shadow is one of the forces that shape our identity, whether we like it or not, whether we claim it or not. As part of our development journey— the journey to self—we each must go down and in, own our shadow, and learn to embrace it as part of ourselves rather than to deny it or disclaim it. If we do not take this inner journey, this part of self will continue to interfere with our attempts to be involved in the activity of leadership. (The concept of shadow, and the importance of the journey toward it, is so important to understanding the self engaged in leadership activities that I describe it in detail in the next chapter.)

Understanding our identity—locating self at the intersection where the various forces meet—requires introspection and reflection, deep inner work, the kind of work that appears as threatening as it does promising. It is not the work that those who live primarily in the external world are used to doing. It also requires honest engagement with others, involvement in relationships in which we risk being vulnerable, open to being wounded and healed, and thus open to learning about ourselves. We understand identity from the inside out, and from the outside in.

Locating Ourselves on the Dependence-Interdependence Continuum

Another aspect of ourselves that is important to partnership-as-leadership is knowing who we are and where we are on the dependence-interdependence continuum. In Psychology 101 we learned that we usually move from dependence to counterdependence to independence to interdependence. This movement can most easily be observed as we watch children become adolescents and adolescents move into adulthood. It is a normal and healthy evolutionary movement, one that is important for individuals to take. It helps in the process of individuation, becoming a separate person with a unique identity, and it helps meet the need for connectedness. It is a basic and simple concept, but one that is important to understanding how identity relates to partnership.

Its importance is this: individuals sometimes get stuck on a particular stretch of the development journey. Some get stuck being dependent, so much so that they give up their identity to accommodate the needs of others. Dependency needs are driven by the need for acceptance and approval, the need to maintain harmony, the need for recognition. The end result of abandoning oneself is that the self is lost. In recent years, the word *codependent* has entered our lexicon as a way of describing those who have lost their self.

Individuals who have lost their self find it difficult, if not impossible, to participate in partnership-as-leadership. They continue to look for strong, heroic leaders who will take care of them. In response to command-and-control leaders, these individuals tend to submit, go along, do what they are told (and often only what they are told), and stay out of trouble.

Others get stuck in counterdependence. Counterdependent individuals tend to distrust authority figures (including bosses) and often do the opposite of what is expected. Counterdependence is a healthy and important phase for adolescents to go through as they develop their own identity separate from that of their parents, and even in work settings counterdependency may occasionally be important to protect oneself from an overbearing, autocratic boss. But some individuals remain counterdependent even though it is no longer helpful or useful. Because executives-as-leaders are in positions of authority, followers stuck in counterdependence fight back, even when fighting back is not appropriate. Counterdependent individuals often find it difficult to engage in partnerships. They suspiciously view it as just another way for command-and-control leaders to manipulate and control.

Individuals stuck in independence can be characterized as tough-minded, take-care-of-myself people. They like autonomy. They welcome authority and responsibility. They like being in charge, setting strategy, giving direction. The idea of strong, heroic leaders makes sense to them. They don't like the idea of dependence, nor (often) the people they see as dependent. Most likely, they also have trouble with the idea of interdependence that provides the foundation for partnership; it appears too soft, even wrongheaded, to them.

Partnership-as-leadership requires that individuals act interdependently. Being interdependent arises from the premise that individuals need each other in the activity of leadership, that no one person can do leadership alone. It is part of a larger supposition that work can no longer be done independently, that any individual needs the active involvement of others if he or she is to accomplish the work. As we move from silos to matrixed organizations, from hierarchy to flatter structures, from fear-based to trust-based organizations, the need for individuals who can and will act interdependently grows stronger. One distinction often made between teams and workgroups is that teams have task interdependence; teamwork is required for the agenda to be completed and the mission fulfilled. Knowing how to work interdependently is a necessity, not an option, in partnerships.

Although the movement from dependence to interdependence is somewhat of a linear journey during the early years of life, adults learn that the movement is not one-time or linear. Moving to a new job, adding significant new challenges to a present job, and welcoming a new boss are several of the events that influence people to move one way or another on the dependence-counterdependence continuum. In addition, individuals can be interdependent in some relationships and dependent in others. Wherever we find ourselves on this continuum, it is important that in any given activity of leadership we know the self that is engaged. It is equally important that we continue our journey toward interdependence.

Claiming Our Gifts

Another part of becoming ourselves comes with understanding and claiming our gifts. Each of us has a gift, a unique and native talent, a talent with which we are born, a talent that can be nurtured and developed. A gift is something you *have* (that is, possess) to contribute to work and to the activity of leadership; once discerned, it is something you *have to* (that is, must) contribute.

Joseph Campbell famously told you to "follow your bliss." I think we do this whenever we claim and use our gifts. But I have noticed that for many people the primary issue is not following their bliss; the issue is knowing or discerning the gift. We often recognize the gifts of others more easily than we can recognize our own native talents.

It is hard to discern our gifts primarily because they are so much a part of who we are. The gift each of us has is so integral to our being and doing, and so integrated into our ways of being and doing, that we fail to notice or nurture it. The gift is part of us, so much so that it helps shape our identity, yet precisely because this is true we often fail to discern it.

It is also difficult to discern and claim our gifts because we live with a belief that anything worthwhile must be earned. This belief derives from some of the early commandments of parents and parent-figures during our childhood. Anything worth doing, we were told, requires effort, if not struggle. In school we worked hard to develop our minds. We sweated through exams, but it was OK because we had this deep-down belief that whatever is tough to learn is truly important. We entered the workforce and realized that there were important skills we did not have, and we worked hard to develop them. Because we were intentional about developing them, we are more aware of them, and they become relatively more important than our gifts. These acquired skills eventually become so important to us that we often base job and career decisions on skills we have learned rather than on the talents that are part of our birthright.

Here is the clearest way I know to discern your gift: think of something you have always known how to do, yet you don't remember spending time or effort learning how to do it. It is something you have always been able to do, and do somewhat effortlessly. Is it coming up with a creative idea? Or is it in synthesizing the ideas of others? Is it your talent in organizing work? Is writing something you do well and don't ever remember learning how to do? Instead of having stage fright, have you always enjoyed acting or speaking in front of others? Each of us has mastery in something, and one part of becoming ourselves—who we started out to be—is to understand, appreciate, and claim that gift.

Gifts are different from knowledge and skills. Our gifts are not acquired; they are part of us. We may choose to nurture them, but we don't sweat in learning them. The challenge with knowledge and skills is in developing them; the challenge in gifts is discerning and claiming them.

Jane's story is a good example of just how important gifts are to leadership and spirit. She joined her organization as a part-time telephone receptionist, a job she sought as she sorted through what she wanted to do with her life and career. When she decided to work full-time, her organization offered her a job as a data-entry clerk. This was not a job that used her gift; it was not even a position for which she had the necessary skills. But they were skills that could be learned, and with patience and hard work Jane learned to do the data entry, and she did it well. She was productive and effective. She was cooperative and client-focused. But she was not inspired, nor was she using all of her energies in her work. Like so many of us, she was doing work she had learned to do, not work that required the use of her gift. She left work each day knowing she had done important work well, but she left feeling unfulfilled.

Some time later, she applied for and got a position as part of a marketing team in the same organization. This job was a better fit for her native talent. It engaged more of her energies. It allowed her to use her gift, at least once in a while. Her performance was still rock solid, but she was more joyful, had more fun, engaged more of her energies at work, and worked with more passion and commitment. More often than not, she left work feeling fulfilled. This job was better; a deeper identity was emerging from within, but she still wasn't fully using her gift.

A year later, in the same organization, Jane joined a team charged with responsibility for developing and distributing a new publication for the organization. She was part of the task force because of her role on the marketing team. When the group got to the point of considering a cover for the publication, the discussion focused on graphic artists the organization had used in the past and could use again. One member of the task force, who knew something of Jane's gift, encouraged her to do the artwork. She was surprised it was suggested but somewhat reluctantly agreed to do it. Doing this artwork was not part of her job description; it was, though, a use of her gift. She spent untold hours, many of them away from work, including evenings and weekends, drawing possible covers. The task required the use of all her energies—mental, physical, emotional, and spiritual. She responded with inspired and creative drawings. The organization could not have paid her for the time, energy, commitment—for the self—that she put into this work. She used her gift and gave the organization a gift in turn.

The team Jane was part of is a good example of how an individual can use her gift in the activity of leadership if leadership is understood as *people working interdependently toward a shared goal.* There was no boss. Instead, leadership happened as a result of the reciprocal relationships among team members, a relationship in which the diversity of gifts brought by each team member was honored. It is also a good example of what happens when we use our gifts in the activity of leadership: we are energized, do inspired work, and in the process lift the spirit of other members of the team.

Each of us has a gift or native talent to contribute to the activity of leadership. But whenever *leadership* is synonymous with *executive,* the few rather than the many get an opportunity to offer their gift. If leadership is understood as partnership, diverse gifts are honored and used, the reciprocity within the relationship is richer and more complete, the results of the leadership activity are more likely to be creative and compelling, and commitment is engendered. Organizations can no longer afford to use the gifts of only a select few; they need to use the diverse gifts held by the many.

It is important that each of us claim and use our gift:

- It is a primary contribution that we can make to the activity of leadership
- Claiming and using the gift is a source of personal power
- Claiming and using it is linked to spirit; we experience a "breath of life," a renewed source of energy, as we use our gift

Heeding Our Call

Call may seem a strange word to use in a book about leadership and business. It is a word usually reserved for those entering full-time religious vocation. But call (or calling) is an important concept for all of us. I include it in this chapter because call is directly related to identity, to becoming who we are, to making our destiny manifest. In *Demian*, Herman Hesse says: "Each person has only one vocation—to find the way to himself. His task is to discover his own destiny—not an arbitrary one—and to live it out wholly and resolutely within himself" (1965, p. 108). Our calling is to discover our identity and to use our gifts to make our destiny manifest.

Though often defined and discussed in supernatural terms, especially when applied to those called into religious vocation, calling can easily be understood as a secular and natural concept. Heeding our call is discerning our gifts and using them such that we meet a need that exists. It is, as Frederick Buechner says, finding that place where our "deep gladness" meets the "world's great hunger." It is just that simple—and just that complex.

Rather than heed this calling, some individuals get caught in the tyranny of the oughts. They spend their work lives doing what they feel they should or ought to do, or what others expect them to do, rather than using their gifts in a way that would be meaningful to them. The stories are legion: the young woman who loves the out-of-doors and wants to become a forest ranger but instead becomes a doctor because her parents and teachers convince her that this is her destiny; a young man whose gift is dance but who chooses to major in business because others tell him he needs to do something practical; the woman who was a brilliant engineer and manager but chooses to forgo a career because of the expectations of others that she stay at home with her young children (the reverse of this also happens; gifted parents choose to work because of pressure from others); the young man who is a talented research scientist and loves "being on the bench" but chooses the management track after being told time and again that the company needs to groom people like him for executive positions. Parker Palmer points out the problem with falling victim to the tyranny of the oughts: "When I follow only the oughts, I may find myself doing work that is ethically laudable but not mine to do. A vocation that is not mine, no matter how externally valued, does violence to the self—in the precise sense that it violates my identity and integrity for some abstract norm. When I violate myself, I invariably violate the people I work with" (1998a, p. 30).

One of the ways I have found that many of us fall victim to the tyranny of the oughts is when we decide to leave the work to which we feel called—work that is a good use of our native talents—to enter the management ranks of an organization. This is the story of the talented research scientist I've just mentioned. It is the story of the brilliant engineer who loves her work but who heeds the company's request to move into management. It is the story of the salesperson who loves "doing deals" but chooses to manage others—who now gets to work with customers and close the contracts. It is the story of the women and men I have met, and with whom I have worked, who have a corner office and with it all the prestige and status they could want but are miserable. For some, managing is a good use of talents and gifts; they heed their callings and are fulfilled in management roles. For others, it is not. It is an ought, one that is rewarded and reinforced by the organization.

To heed our call is to decide to use our native gifts and talents, to do the things we know how to do and do well, rather than falling victim to the tyranny of the oughts. It is following our bliss rather than the supposed bliss that someone else holds out in front of us. It is going with our grain rather than against it. There are times when we must go against our grain, to develop new skills and perspectives; one of those times is when we go against our grain to develop the capacities we need to fully engage in partnerships. But it is also important that we remember our calling and use our gifts.

Partnerships allow people to heed their calling and still use their native talents in activities of leadership. In partnership-as-leadership, it is not just those in the corner office who exercise leadership but all the individuals who have opportunities to use their gifts to help accomplish the shared goals of the organization. In fact, partnerships require that all the people use their gifts. I suggest that when individuals heed their call and are given opportunities to engage in partnership-as-leadership even though they are not in the executive suite, they are happier and more fulfilled and their organization is more productive.

Other individuals work in order to survive. They work because it is essential. They don't find deep gladness in it. They find no deep joy in the process. Instead, work is numbing and stifling. They endure weekdays because weekends are coming. One sure sign of this is the number of workers who still see Wednesday as "hump day": if they can just get through Wednesday, they are more than halfway to another two days off from the drudgery called work. There is no fulfillment in work, no sense that spiritual energy can be used in it.

It is hard to participate in partnerships when operating on our oughts or working only to survive. Operating on our oughts is not the way to make our vision manifest; it is not the path toward the experience of deep gladness. Living for the weekends reveals that we are working at something that is dispiriting, that takes energy from us and sucks life out of us. We hope to be ourselves away from work because we are not ourselves at work. In either case, we have little of ourself to contribute to the activity of leadership. Our organizations suffer; and so do we.

But if we heed our calling, if we claim our gifts and use them to find "deep gladness" in the work we do, then our work is our vocation, and we have our real and whole self to contribute to the activity of leadership. Our organizations are enhanced, and so are we.

Being Whole Men and Women

Earlier, I described the four energies that are part of each of us: the mental, the physical, the emotional, and the spiritual. We are a combination of all four energies. To become the person we started out to be, to become our whole selves, we must claim and use all these energies.

We are most aware of our mental and physical energy. Work requires that we use them; our organizations expect and reward them. We have long understood the link between mental and physical energy, between thoughts and behavior. We believe that one affects, and is affected by, the other.

Most leadership development efforts, in and outside the places where we work, have focused on developing more effective leadership behaviors or on developing new knowledge, but not on helping us become who we started out to be and on learning to honor and use all of our energies in our work. We link mental and physical energy, but emotional energy—and to an even greater extent spiritual energy—is not often included in this interdependent link.

Two assumptions, each discussed earlier in this book, provide part of its foundation. First, we have four energies, one of which is the spiritual. Second, we are whole people who cannot be fragmented and compartmentalized. Part of our identity is spiritual. To be fully alive and fully human, we must claim our spiritual energy, understand the integration and interdependence of all of our energies, and use all of them in our work and in the activity of leadership.

Using spiritual energy means being human, being fully human, as opposed to, say, evolving to some higher form of existence. It is a completely natural concept, not a supernatural one. Understanding and making room for spirit extends to us a different source of energy or breath of life than what we get from the other three. This energy is important for us to have and to invest in the activity of leadership. More important, we cannot be whole men and women without using all our energies. It is time to unmask and uncover spirit; it is part of our real self.

Being Authentic

In a word, to be authentic is to be our real selves in the external world.

Being authentic is knowing ourselves and being ourselves as we engage with others in the activity of leadership—no playing roles, no acting, no fulfilling the expectations of others. We are actually and exactly who we are. Nothing false, nothing imitative, nothing imaginary. Being authentic means not hiding behind a mask, not faking what we think or feel, not using spin to promote a sanitized version of the truth. Being authentic is living with honesty and integrity. It is being transparent and congruent, matching inner reality with its outward expression.

Being authentic is hard. Early in life, we learn we cannot be authentic and please the important adults in our life.

We are taught not to feel what we feel. "Big kids don't cry"; "You know you love your little sister; tell her you're sorry"; "You know you like broccoli."

We are taught not to say what we see or think. "It is not nice to say that man is bald"; "You shouldn't say that Grandmother's house has a funny smell."

We are taught not to ask for what we want. "It is not nice to ask for a soft drink. Always wait until it is offered."

We are taught not to act so as to take care of ourselves. "We should share our toys and always let company play with the toys first."

Part of the process of socialization is to learn to keep some feelings hidden, not speak the truth we see or think, and act in un-self-ish ways. The injunctions we receive from parents and other significant adults about what to feel and think and how to act are most often well intended and sometimes appropriate. They are designed to help us get along well in civilized society. But the problem is that we learn to project a false self, not to live or speak our truth.

Projecting a false self is reinforced in the places we work. Too often, we learn the importance of telling others, especially the bosses for whom we work, what they want to hear. We learn to fudge the truth, or at least not tell all of it. We learn to play political games, learn how to leave a CYA paper trail. We learn that collusion is easier, and often more welcomed, than courage.

Not all of our collusion comes from what we say or do. It sometimes comes from our passivity or disengagement. We don't speak up when a colleague is being unfairly maligned, we remain silent when a decision to "go to Abilene" is being made, we stay detached from the politics of the organization because we don't want to get our hands dirty. Being passive and detached is another way of projecting a false self.

We feed the false self, Angeles Arrien suggests, "by editing our thoughts, rehearsing our emotions, performing what we think other people want to see, or hiding our true selves. We feed the false-self system whenever we are unwilling to tell the truth, say what is so, or give voice to what we see" (1993, p. 94). At the same time, being authentic is not a license to demean, discount, or dispirit. Under the guise of being honest, we often do just that. What we call truth telling is full of blame and judgment. In the work I do, I teach individuals how to give and receive feedback that is intended to help them understand how their behavior has an impact on others. It is important that those who give feedback be honest, describe the situation, relate what they saw or experienced, and identify the emotional impact it had on them ("I felt left out," "I was disappointed"). The norm we suggest to those giving feedback is that they be "totally honest" and "totally kind." This is the authenticity we each need to learn and practice.

Identity and authenticity are closely linked. Identity is understanding the self that is at the intersection of the forces that shape us; authenticity is being that real self in all aspects of life. Being authentic honors our being, our real and true self. It creates—or, as the case may be, restores—trust. It enables us to experience the force we call spirit; we are renewed and revitalized whenever we have the courage to be authentic. It makes leadership-as-partnership possible.

Identity and Shadow

The concept of the shadow has been briefly mentioned in this chapter and in Chapter Three. Understanding the shadow, and learning to embrace it, is critical to our understanding and acceptance of our identity, of our whole self; it is essential to understanding and practicing partnership-as-leadership. In the next chapter, the concept of the shadow and its relationship to identity and to partnerships is explored in depth.

Chapter Six

Developing Our Inner Life

Leaders, in the very way they become leaders, tend
to screen out their inner consciousness.
—Parker Palmer (1998b, p. 6)

We cannot afford the luxury of silence about the
spiritual condition of our leaders. They themselves
are experiencing stresses at a deep personal level
which many of them cannot cope with; and they
are taking action in their organizations that reflect
their fragile and embattled spiritual condition.
—Peter Vaill (1998, p. 217)

Of all the "soft stuff" that executives and managers, and all of the
rest of us, try to avoid, inner consciousness may be the softest of
all. Inner consciousness cannot be quantified. It cannot be studied empirically. It cannot be experienced by any of the senses. It
is not part of the curriculum at the Harvard Business School. It is
hard to understand, much less appreciate. Managers and executives have enough problems and issues with which to wrestle;
they see no need to go on an inner journey to find more. Plus, the
part of the journey to our self that takes us in and down is the
most difficult part to traverse, let alone complete. It is, then,
rather easy to dismiss inner consciousness as not the right stuff to
deal with. It is easier to operate on the belief that what you see is
what you get.

Inner Life Affects Outer Work

Added to the problem is that most of us are only dimly aware of how what goes on deep inside affects our involvement, for good or bad, in leadership activities. We do not know what we project from deep within us onto relationships and organizations. Yet all of my experience, both personal and professional, convinces me that inner life and outer work are inextricably linked. What you see is *not* all of what you get. Unwittingly and unintentionally, we project what goes on in our depths onto all of our outer experiences, including our practices of leadership. What we project is not always benign; sometimes it is toxic—to ourselves, to others, and to our organizations.

Focusing only on the external world—that which is material and has substance—costs individuals and organizations. We lose touch with deep sources of passion and creativity, spend vital energy maintaining a front, and never find the hidden wholeness that awaits us. Worse, we spend our lives haunted by those parts of the self that we try to repress or deny. Worse still, truths about the self don't stay buried. We cannot keep them in our underground; they surface to hurt us and others at all the wrong times.

There is also a cost to organizations. Organizations carry those parts of the inner life of executives and managers that have been projected onto it—their fears, their insecurities, their pain—and it has a negative impact. In Chapter Three, I wrote about the shadow side of executives with whom I have worked closely in recent years: one anger-based, one fear-based, one approval-based. None of the three focused on inner consciousness. In today's parlance, they "didn't want to go there." They all seemed unaware of how they projected their shadows onto the organizations they headed and of the consequences for the organizations. But they did project, and it did cost. The fear of the second executive, for example, became pervasive throughout the organization. I have never been in an organization where more people were more fearful. They watched what they said, left unnecessary paper trails, would not speak their truth.

Other managers, some from two and three levels down the hierarchy, called the CEO paranoid, but in truth they too acted just as fearfully. The CEO's fear was pervasive and toxic, not just harming him and the senior managers but creating unhealthy people and an unhealthy organization. The collective shadow of this organization, the pervasive fear and paranoia that for the most part was truly undiscussible, is a disowned part of the chief executive, projected onto the organization.

More recently, I had another opportunity to learn of the costs of an unexamined inner life. I was serving as an executive coach for the four top executives of a national organization located in the Southwest. To prepare for the one-to-one coaching, I gathered extensive data from interviews with those who knew these executives well, and then added data from a multirater feedback instrument to fill out the picture that emerged from the interviews. To put what I learned simply: one of the executives had a lot of insecurity and fear in his shadow, and another had a lot of anger in hers.

The fear and insecurity showed itself in the first executive's unwillingness to deal with even the simplest of conflicts, and his unwillingness to make difficult decisions even after all the data were in. He sent performance appraisals and information about salary increases through registered mail; face-to-face conversations were not in the offing. Though he needed to represent his organization in the larger business community, he was not comfortable in meeting or dealing with others who had similar positions in other organizations.

But it wasn't just the executive who felt deep-down insecurity. The organization carried it as well, projected from the executive. This unexamined insecurity was toxic to the executive; it kept him from using all of his energy in his work and kept him from being a free and whole person. It was also toxic to the organization; too much organizational energy was spent struggling with the shared sense of insecurity rather than spent in the needed service that is core to its mission.

The woman executive could turn even the smallest thing into a major confrontation. But she didn't always do so, and this was part of the problem. At one moment she would be warm and charming; the next, she could be accusatory, demeaning, angry. She could get so angry that she would actually throw things in meetings—never hitting anyone, but scaring everyone. Feedback from a multirater instrument confirmed this: she was more forceful than enabling, more tough than compassionate, more aggressive than supportive. Her anger, I suspect, was based on some deep-down fears: fear of not being in control, fear of natural chaos, fear that others were not as bright or as committed as she and thus that she had to be responsible for everything. None of those who worked most closely with her would say she was fearful; it was not evident. Anger was, but fear wasn't. But the fear was evident in the organization; this was where the executive had projected it. Individual men and women expended enormous energy managing this fear. The cost to them and the organization was great.

Neither of these executives were self-aware. Neither had taken a journey in and down to discover how the inner life affected outer work. They did not know that others breathed a sigh of relief whenever they left town on vacation or business. Even I noticed the difference in the environment when they were not around; employees were more relaxed, more energized, more vitalized.

There is another cost to this organization. As David Whyte, poet and author, puts it: "If the corporation ignores the darker underbelly of their employee's lives (including but not limited to the lives of executives) for a well-meaning approach, emphasizing only the positive, they will be forced to rely on expensive management pyramids to manipulate their workers at the price of commitment" (1994, p. 7). The understanding and practice of partnership is based on commitment rather than control, collaboration rather than competition, and trust and openness rather than manipulation. None of these are possible if we don't acknowledge—and even embrace—our darker underbelly. So long as we project the stuff going on in our depths onto relationships, true partnerships are not possible, and management pyramids seem necessary.

If the costs are so great, why do we screen out our inner consciousness? Why don't we take the journey in and down to examine our inner lives? I have wondered about these questions a lot and reflected on them in terms of my own experience.

For some twenty years, and until I moved into a new role several years ago, I had increasingly significant management responsibilities in two organizations. The first of my two management jobs was with one of the operating companies of Atlantic Richfield, and the other was as director of the products group at the Center for Creative Leadership. In this last position, the group had significant "profit-and-loss" responsibility (I put this in quotes because as a nonprofit organization the center has no profit; still, we had to make income in excess of expenses every year), and I reported directly to the president and was part of the executive management team.

Like most of the managers and executives with whom I have been privileged to work during my career, I spent most of my time and energy as a manager and leader focused on the externals. As I indicated in an earlier chapter, I prefer to deal with those things that can be known to the senses. I am more of a realist than an idealist, and I like dealing in the here and now rather some future possibility. (Fortunately for me, there were others in the group who had strengths in developing new ideas and imagining future scenarios.) Because of these preferences, I focused on things that were tangible and concrete: goals and objectives, budgets, securing and allocating resources, solving problems, and putting out brush fires.

So one of the reasons I did not spend time on issues of the inner life was that it simply did not occur to me to do so. Perhaps it hasn't occurred to you to do so, either. Nothing in my formal education process or my work experience suggested the need for it. No boss recommended it during any formal or informal performance-appraisal process. Only a few of the development courses in which I participated ever remotely suggested it. Even my awareness of how my inner life was having an impact on my outer work was a faint one; to the extent I suspected anything, I thought for sure that I could keep it underground.

Now, in retrospect, I know another reason I did not focus on inner life. It just seemed too hard, too scary. At those times I would get close, I'd back off. I would read something occasionally, even talk about the inner life with friends, but I kept it at a safe, cognitive level. It was OK to try to understand it, but not to experience it. Parker Palmer describes why I was thinking and feeling this way: "Everything in us cries out against it [it being an inner journey]. That's why we externalize everything. It's easier to deal with the external world. It is easier to spend your life manipulating an institution than it is dealing with your own soul. It truly is. We make institutions sound complicated and hard and rigorous, but they are a piece of cake compared to our inner workings" (1998b, p. 202).

It took two experiences (which researchers at the Center for Creative Leadership have labeled "hardships"; more on this later) to nudge me into an inner journey, at least the part of it that I have been on thus far.

In my first significant managerial job, I moved to a new state, into a job that had high stakes, in which my predecessor had failed, a job that one of my new direct reports felt he deserved and should have gotten. My relationship with him was strained, tense, and contentious. But I was determined to make it better; I was sure that with time and the interpersonal skills I had I could. I pondered often and deeply what I could do to build an effective working relationship with him. I talked to and got advice from a lot of different people. I tried a number of strategies. Along the way, I realized that some of my stuff—what was going on deep inside of me—was getting in the way, that my inner life was affecting our relationship. It was the first time that this reality became crystal clear to me.

The personal trauma that influenced me to go on an inner journey was a divorce. Like no other experience in my life, this divorce, and the counseling that I engaged in at that time, brought me face-to-face with the monsters that dwell within me: my insecurities, my fears, my dependencies. The therapist with whom I worked was the first person to encourage me to embrace my monsters rather than deny, repress, or project them. At first, I resisted the idea; I wanted to get rid of them. Over time, and with her support and encouragement, I began the process of accepting the truth that the monsters were an important part of me and that I could befriend them. The process of embracing the monsters is not finished; it is ongoing work for me.

From both of these experiences, and others like them, I realize that one of my monsters is fear of losing control, fear of work and life becoming chaotic. I organize everything, from my office at work to my closet at home. I plan everything, want nothing left to chance, whether it's where we will stay on vacation next month to how we will staff programs next year. I make to-do lists, one for home and one for the office—and I do it for reasons other than helping me remember things. Doing so helps me maintain my illusion that I have things under control; I don't feel as anxious or fearful that something won't get done. Colleagues at work call me compulsive ("From inside me looking out, it looks normal," I usually reply), and one of my daughters at home, in a way that only she could do, calls me anal.

Being anal has some advantages. Reports get sent, proposals made, recommendations completed, and problems solved in a timely fashion. I know where things are. I am never late for anything. Few things fall through the cracks. Some people even compliment me for my neat and orderly office (though they probably would not want to work in such a sterile environment). But my fear of being out of control and my penchant for organizing does not leave much room for spontaneity in life or work. I am not as adaptable or flexible as I would like to be or as I sometimes need to be. I know that creativity comes out of chaos, and thus I also know that my attempts to control things too much squelch creativity. Whenever I am not aware of this fear, I project it onto others, and in the process I negatively affect them and our relationships.

What you see is not what you get. Inner life affects outer work.

Inner Life and the Shadow

We are a tapestry. On the front side of the tapestry that is us, the threads are woven together beautifully. From this side of ourselves, we cast light and foster connectedness. We trust others. We work collaboratively and develop partnership-as-leadership. This is the part of ourselves that we hope others see, the part we are glad to show in public. It is our persona. On the back side of the tapestry, there are knots—not pretty, but part of the essence of the tapestry. It isn't possible to have the front side without the back. From the back side (or, if you want, from the dark underbelly), we cast our shadows and foster disconnection. The dark underbelly is home to our fears, our envies, our dependencies, our anger—things often part of our unconscious. To the extent that we are aware of things lurking in the shadow, we try to repress them, or deny they are there, or project them on to someone else. For sure, we don't want to claim them as part of ourselves.

Jung told us that the shadow is part of each of us. We each "carry a shadow"; none of us is exempt. Throughout our lives, what goes on deep inside remains attached to us like a shadow. It is the part of us that we do not wish to be, the part that the ego tries to keep hidden from others. What exists in the shadow runs counter to our conscious ideals. As the stories I have told suggest, the shadow is home to our fears, anxieties, insecurities.

The paradox is that the more we try to hide the back side of the tapestry or escape the shadow, the more we are imprisoned by it. Jung told us what each of us must learn from our experience: our shadow becomes more beastlike if we try to deny it or hide it, and then this beast winds up hurting us and others deeply.

One part of our development journey is to take an inner journey, identify the shadow, and find our whole self on the other side of it. Alan Briskin says that when we go in and down and find a shadow, it is like "finding a stranger in one's own home" (1996, p. 2). It is a stranger we don't want to find there, and don't particularly care to meet. But it is a stranger who is our self, at least in part. Jung suggested that when we finally greet this stranger, our question should not be "How do I get rid of you?" but rather "How can I claim you?" or even "How do I embrace you?"

The shadow's companion is the persona, that part of ourselves that we show in public, that we let others know and see. It is our persona that makes polite and civilized discourse, even social relationships, possible. Often we delude ourselves into thinking that we are only the persona—our public self—that we want to be and want others to know. Because our persona is also part of us, we try to operate with the belief that "what you see is all there is."

So, what exists in the shadow? What strangers might we find on our inner journey? I have previously mentioned three of them in stories I told about the anger-based, fear-based, and approval-based executives. But there are others.

During the time I was responsible for management and organization development in a major corporation, one of my internal clients was responsible for a huge operation. He was a brilliant engineer, knowledgeable, forceful, influential, and by all external measures successful. Away from work, he was fun to be with, the life of the party in a relaxed and joyful way. He appeared confident and self-assured; he had no problems making tough decisions, confronting people whose work was unacceptable, even taking on corporate when he disagreed with a decision being handed down. Few people would have thought of him as having a problem with insecurity. But as I observed him over a period of several years, as I noticed how much he needed to let others know that he was the boss, as I realized how often he kept others in a one-down position (he wanted compliance, not collaboration) and how he used coercive power to keep them there, the more I began to think that if I could peel back several layers I would find an insecure, threatened man. He did not appear to know this about himself; it was part of his shadow. His shadow wasn't benign, it was toxic. It poisoned him, it poisoned others, and it poisoned relationships.

Other managers and executives share another particular type of insecurity or anxiety: I call it the impostor syndrome (I regret not knowing whom to credit for this phrase; I wish I had). Much of the work I do is feedback-intensive. It is helping managers and executives—all leaders in one way or another—get a good fix on who they are through various kinds of assessment. They learn about their strengths, their development needs, their impact on others, and their personal preferences—what makes them tick. It is leadership development as development of the person. It is leadership development from the inside out. Many share a fear that during the intensive assessment process they will be "found out," a fear that comedian Robin Williams described in a recent interview: "The essential truth is that sometimes you're worried that they will find out it's a fluke, that you don't really have it. You've lost the muse or—worst dread—you never had it at all. I went through all that madness early on" (Rader, 1998, p. 4). Like other aspects of the shadow, this fear can feel like madness. It is madness that infects us, and it infects others.

Parker Palmer (though I have never met him, he is one of my favorite "teachers"; I like nothing better than to spend an afternoon engaging in discourse with him while reading something he's written—his writings invite dialogue) has identified five monsters that exist within the shadow of leaders (1998b).

First is the shadow of insecurity about identity, about one's worth as a person. For many of us (Palmer says he sees it especially in men), our identity is so tied to our title and our job, and our insecurity is so great, that if we were to lose our title or job we would lose our sense of self. How does this get projected? Palmer writes that "these leaders create institutional settings that deprive other people of their identity as a way of dealing with the unexamined fears in the leaders themselves" (p. 204). It is difficult for men or women whose identity is tied up in a title, in the status symbols that accompany high positions of great authority, or in a particular job to move to a more collaborative, partnership model of leadership. For them, it would be like losing their identity.

The second shadow that Palmer sees in leaders is the inner fear that the universe is essentially hostile and life is a battle. "We talk about tactics and strategies, about using 'our big guns', about 'do or die', about wins and losses" (p. 205). Because we fear that this is the way life is, we choose competition over collaboration; we create situations that are win-lose; and we develop relationships that are one-up, one-down. Because of this fear, individuals hang onto their coercive power (after all, they need it to win) and continue to favor hierarchy and bureaucracy more than community. This may be what is motivating the fear-based and insecurity-based executives described earlier. Like other aspects of our shadows, this fear may only be dimly recognized, yet it deeply affects how we relate and how we engage in leadership activities.

The third aspect of shadow Palmer names is "functional atheism." It is the deep-down belief that the "ultimate responsibility for everything rests with me . . . it is the unexamined conviction that if anything decent is going to happen, I am the one who needs to make it happen here" (p. 205). This belief, and the action we take based on it, obviously leads to stress and burnout for the individual, as well as leading to unhealthy and unproductive relationships with those with whom we work. Less obviously, it is not possible to enact partnership-as-leadership so long as an executive carries a deeply held conviction that ultimate responsibility rests with him or her, that the buck must always finally stop at his or her door.

The fear of the natural chaos of life is the fourth inner reality that Palmer identified as lurking in the shadow. "I think that a lot of leaders become leaders because they have a lifelong devotion to eliminating all remnants of chaos from the world," Palmer writes (p. 206). As soon as I read this, I knew he was describing me. As I suggested earlier, I try to control chaos in my own world, if not the entire world. I attempt to organize and structure everything; doing so protects my illusion that I am in control. I have worked with other executives who have the same fear. One was so fearful of ambiguity and chaos that she tried to develop a standard operating procedure for every possible situation that might arise in her department. She wanted nothing left to chance—or even to the judgment of other individuals. For those of us with this fear in our shadows, we project it by creating norms, policies, practices, and SOPs to cover every possible situation.

The final example of a shadow that leaders (read this as all of us) project on others, Palmer suggests, is the denial of death. This is demonstrated, he suggests, in how we try to keep everything alive, including projects, programs, and people who have been in a coma for years but have never been laid to rest. This fear is related to partnership in that we do not move to this practice of leadership until we recognize that we live in a postheroic age and that it is OK to let go of old ways of being leaders and doing leadership.

Read all this and it is easy to begin to believe that the shadow is the bad or evil side of us. It isn't. It is the comparatively primitive and unadapted side. Jung's way of saying this was that it contained more of our basic animal nature. But the shadow also helps us be more spontaneous, creative, and childlike. The shadow helps us experience strong emotions. It adds zest and vitality to life. It adds breadth and depth to life. Our hope and our task is not to rid ourselves of the shadow but rather to engage in processes in which we move things lurking in the shadow from the unconscious to our conscious and begin to embrace them. As we embrace them, we stop projecting them. We become more whole, freer to participate fully in the activity of leadership, more open to spirit working in and through us in shaping our identity. In our outer lives, we are better able to understand and accept others, including things lurking in *their* shadow, and we are better able to engage in partnerships.

The Journey Inward: Embracing Our Shadow

Learning to embrace our shadow is a journey down and in that inevitably leads to a meeting with a new part of ourselves, a journey for which there is no guaranteed rite of passage. It is a journey that some avoid all of their lives, or at least as long as their egos can repress the shadow or they can project everything negative onto others. Others start the journey and then turn back. To fully commit to an inner journey is a test of our courage. Jung said that "this confrontation [with self] is the first test of courage on the inner way, a test sufficient to frighten off most people, for the meeting with ourselves belongs to the more unpleasant things that can be avoided so long as we can project everything negative into the environment" (1993, p. 381).

So, why take this journey? Simply, it is the only way to get to where we want to be. Let me remind you of a story as a way of making this point. I love Old Testament stories. They are so real—real people struggling with real-life issues. One of my favorites is the story of the Exodus event. It is a story that can be read on several levels. On one level, it is a story of the journey that each of us must take, a journey from bondage through the wilderness to Canaan, a land flowing with milk and honey. Most of us would like to leave behind the things that imprison and bind us; we would like to get to the point where we don't project our shadow onto relationships and organizations. Our deep wish, though, is to find a way to do this—to get to the promised land—that does not involve wilderness wanderings. We are willing to walk around the wilderness, and often we walk up to its edge to see if there isn't some way around it. But we don't want to walk through it. Why not avoid the pain, the uncertainty, the trouble if we can? None us likes to be torn and tattered by life's experiences. The Exodus story reminds us that there is no way around the wilderness; the way out is in and through.

The Exodus story also reminds us of several of the essential steps in the journey. First, we must acknowledge that the monsters in our shadows—our fears, our insecurities, our anxieties about the world, our dependency needs—keep us in bondage. Until we are aware of being imprisoned, there is no reason to move toward freedom. Sometimes we learn about how shadow constrains us when we experience particularly painful hardships: the loss of a friendship, a failure at work, a midlife divorce, a bout of depression. These experiences nudge us to begin the journey in and down. At other times, we become aware of bondage because of our active involvement in one or more spiritual disciplines. Yet other times, we begin the journey because the spirit that weaves through and permeates all of our experience is always at work within us nudging us toward wholeness. We have a slow but real dawning that the unexamined life is not as full and complete as it might be, and a sense that on the other side of the shadow we will find a more complete self.

The next step in the journey is engaging the wilderness, moving toward the shadow. It is tough to enter the wilderness, to begin the journey in and down, because we don't know what we will find there. But we do know that some monsters—some fears, anxieties, and insecurities—are terrifying. We know too that we will meet the things we hate about ourselves and usually project on others. This is a journey toward one of the most difficult but most important parts of self.

But even after we commit to the wilderness and begin the inner journey, questions remain. If the shadow exists primarily in our unconscious, how can we know it? If we don't know it, how can we move toward it, much less embrace it? Life offers clues about our shadows. We know we are getting close when we become aware of

- Things that tend to set us off. What slights cause you to over-react? When does your anger pop out to haunt you? What about your fears?
- What we don't like in others, especially others of the same sex. It is onto them that we most likely project the shadow.
- Those things we know about ourselves but try to keep hidden, the ways we don't want to be but deep down know we are.
- Our dreams (they are a rich source of clues).
- Feedback from others. Sometimes we learn the truth about ourselves from outside of us.

On the other side of the wilderness is Canaan, a promised land. This is the final step of the journey in and down; it is our intended destination. For our purposes, Canaan is what Thomas Merton called a "hidden wholeness," a place where we experience an internal sense of wholeness and true connectedness to others. It is the promise this place exists that makes the journey worth taking.

Reflection and Action

Through the years, I have read a lot about the inner journeys of others. I am interested in knowing how others go in and down in search of wholeness. I hope that I can learn from their journeys as I take my own. One of the first things I noticed is how some individuals seem to take the journey in and down through contemplation, and they do it alone. They start with reflection. Robert Greenleaf is a good example. Greenleaf, the originator and developer of the concept of servant leadership, preferred to meditate. He even came to view it as one way of serving—the meditation of one person enriched others, he thought. For Greenleaf and others like him, it is after taking this inner journey alone that they are willing or able to actively engage the world, and to do so in a way that makes sense and provides meaning.

On the one hand, I have tried the reflective disciplines, with varying degree of success, but I worried that I didn't seem to have the capacity to do them easily or well. On the other hand, I have always been involved in communities where I lived and worked, and I have become acutely aware that my active engagement in the world has pushed me out of my comfort zone and led me into periods of introspection and reflection. Catalysts for my inner work have been the hardship experiences mentioned earlier, and also active development experiences such as rich and feedback-intensive workshops, relationships that deepened the questions I ask of myself, work experiences that challenged my view that focusing on the externals was enough, and deep dialogue in faith communities. What seems to work for me is action, then reflection. For me, action is a prelude to reflection.

I have long suspected that this difference in starting points is the result of basic personality preferences. Among the contributions that Jung made to what we know of personality is the understanding of basic preferences. Two of these preferences seem to relate to how we take the inner journey. "There are two poles of psychic orientation," write Maggie Hyde and Michael McGuinness in describing Jung's idea; "in the extrovert attitude, energy flows outward to the world and is motivated and oriented by external factors and relationships. Introverted energy withdraws from the world and is motivated and oriented by inner factors" (Hyde and McGuinness, 1994, p. 77). Given this, perhaps extroverts start their inner journeys with action and in relationships and then move to reflection, while introverts start with a form of silence and in solitude and then move to action.

Whatever the starting point, these two poles are inextricably linked. Palmer writes: "A tug-of-war between active and contemplative life has gone on for a long time in the Western world. . . . Contemplation and action ought not be at war with one another. . . . Contemplation and action are not contradictions, but poles of a great paradox . . . one cannot exist without the other. . . . When we fail to hold the paradox together, action flies off into frenzy, a frantic and even violent effort to impose one's will on the world. Contemplation flies off into escapism—a flight from the world into a world of false bliss" (1990, pp. 6, 7, and 15). He is saying that one provides a safeguard for the other. My experience is that one is never complete without the other, and that in fact one feeds the other. Our inner journeys require both.

Practices of Reflection and Action

The purpose of reflection and action is to help us discover (or, if you will, uncover) the truth about ourselves. It is to assist us in getting beyond our persona, the mask we wear in public and change for our various publics, so we can engage the shadow and claim the whole and true self that exists on the other side. Any discipline that helps us do that is an important spiritual discipline.

Reflective Disciplines

Among the reflective disciplines individuals use to do inner work are these four.

Silence. In *The Seven Spiritual Laws of Success*, Deepak Chopra says that one way for us to discover our "essential nature" and "know who you really are" is to learn the practice of silence. "Practicing silence," he says, "means making a commitment to simply be" (1994, p. 14). It means no talking, no reading, no watching TV. It is taking time to listen, and listen deeply, to what life has to say to us. Chopra suggests that we set aside time each day, perhaps a time in the morning and evening, to experience silence.

Meditation. For years, I thought of meditation as something quite mysterious and complex, a practice reserved for a special few rather than something everyone could do. Jon Kabat-Zinn suggests that the opposite is true. "People think of meditation as some kind of special activity," he writes; "but this is not exactly correct. Meditation is simplicity itself. It is about stopping and being present, that is all" (1994, p. 11). Meditation takes many forms, but a good starting point is simply to stop doing and start being who you are where you are. It is to be mindful of our thoughts and feelings in the moment. No evaluation or judging, simply being aware. Kabat-Zinn suggests that paying attention to our breathing, our breathing in and our breathing out, is one way to begin learning to stay in the moment. Meditation helps us become aware of our inner processes, to identify our habits of thought and feeling, to be mindful of what stirs deep within, and to notice how, for example, we overreact to a slight that we experience.

Prayer. Prayer is a form of meditation, just as meditation and prayer can be forms of silence. The distinction among the three is that in moving from silence to meditation to prayer we move from being more passive and receptive to more active. In prayer, there is a time and space for being receptive, but we can go beyond being mindful to giving voice to our fear and insecurities, our hopes and dreams, our concerns for individuals and relationships. Acknowledging and owning our monsters is but one purpose of more active prayers, but digging deep into our inner lives and confessing what we know is there is an important and appropriate use of prayer.

Journaling. Journaling has become an important reflective discipline for me. After I spend time alone with my journal, I am surprised at what I have written. I often start writing about an event or an experience but often wind up dealing with some aspect of my inner life. It was not what I started out to write—not even something I was aware of thinking or feeling. New insights, often deeper insights, come to me as I write. In Jung's terms, I have more of an extroversion attitude toward life, get more of my energy from people and events external to me, often find active disciplines more helpful than reflective ones. Yet journaling has been helpful to me on my journey in and down. One reason this is true, I suspect, is that in journaling I write only for me. I assume that no one else will read what I write, and thus I feel no need to censor any thought or feeling that surfaces.

Through the years, I have asked executives and managers to describe other disciplines they use at work that focus on reflection and solitude. They include the typical disciplines I've mentioned, but also intentional reflection on their involvement in and impact on the events of the workday and -week, using commutes to and from work to reflect and integrate, making space for quiet during the day, and using guided visualizations. There is a lot of variety in the reflective disciplines individuals use.

Active Disciplines

In the mid-1990s Christopher Schaefer and Jeri Darling, principals in the High Tor Alliance for Organization and Community

Renewal, began a study of the disciplines individuals use in work and organizational life to engage their inner life. Those who responded to the survey and later engaged in in-depth interviews reported using many of the practices of reflection suggested here, but they also reported (Schaefer and Darling, 1996) many practices that start with action. Among them are these five.

Sharing of Personal Life Stories. Sharing our life's story is a powerful way to remember experiences and events and people that have had an impact on us, often at a deep level; hearing the life story of another reminds us of aspects of our own that lie buried deep within. My experience in sharing my life story is similar to the one I have in journaling: I am sometimes surprised at what I hear myself saying. Stories help us get beneath the surface, to explore what's going on in our depths.

Deep Listening. Deep listening means being fully present with another person. It involves paying attention to what he or she says with mind, heart, and spirit. It includes being nonjudgmental. Deep listening is a gift to the other person; it helps the person on the journey. It is also a gift to us; we deepen our awareness of ourselves as we listen.

Not long ago, I experienced the gift and power of deep listening while participating in a "clearness committee," a process used in Quaker communities that allows an individual or a couple to bring personal questions or issues to a "committee," that is, other individuals who are committed to being present and listening deeply. The members of the committee cannot prescribe solutions, cannot say what they would do if it were their concern, cannot ask questions to which there is but one right answer. They can and do listen deeply, and they can ask open-ended questions, questions for which they don't have an answer. In the clearness committee in which I was a participant, the process enabled and encouraged the person with the issue to go in and down and discover new truths.

Seeking Feedback.   Sometimes feedback from others is the catalyst for our inner journeys. We are not always self-aware; we don't always know the impact our behavior has on others. We don't always know when our monsters have popped out and hurt others. At times, others know truths about us that we do not know or have not acknowledged. At these times, feedback can be an unfreezing experience, opening us to new and deeper insights about how the inner life and outer work are connected. Understood in this way, feedback can start the journey in and down, even if it doesn't complete it.

Personal Growth Workshops.   Personal growth experiences that foster inner awareness, and that examine the relationship of inner life and outer work, are important experiences in the journey to the self. The topics may vary, from clarifying deeply held personal values and comparing them to organizational values, to creating a personal vision statement, to power and powerlessness. Teaching and learning methods may vary, from intensive one-to-one feedback to use of simulated activities, to use of leaderless group activities. But the focus is the same: helping us think about ourselves, and our involvement in the activity of leadership, from the inside out.

A colleague recently told me about another type of personal growth experience that was the catalyst for her deep inner work. She participated in an eight-day Outward Bound experience, one that she went on in part because she wanted to break new ground in her life. She told me that before she went, her biggest fears were about things external to her: snakes, bugs, wasps. She quickly learned that the source of her worst fears was internal, that the most important conflicts with which she needed to come to grips were rooted deep inside. Some of the fears and conflicts were not part of her conscious awareness; some she was dimly aware of. The activities in which she participated—the ropes course, the overnight done alone, the river trip—brought these feelings to the surface. The activities, the deep reflection she carried out, and the support she received during the process enabled her to go in and down and embrace her shadow.

Work Itself. Our jobs are the classroom in which we come face-to-face with the impact of the inner life on our work, and in this classroom we have the opportunity to learn some of life's most enduring lessons, including lessons about the shadow. It is often some difficult, challenging experience at work—related to the job itself, other people, or a setback—that pushes us out of bondage and into the wilderness, that is the catalyst for our starting the journey in and down.

Other practices reported in the High Tor study that combine action and reflection are jogging, walking in nature, participating in corporate worship, gardening, and engaging in an art form such as pottery making. As reported, these practices were sometimes done alone, sometimes with others.

There is at least one other kind of "action" that encourages us to work on our inner life. In research done at the Center for Creative Leadership on how executives learn, grow, and change over the course of their career, one type of experience from which many individuals reported learning important leadership and life lessons was labeled "hardship." (I reported on two of mine earlier in this chapter.) We learn from loss and suffering. We learn from the mistakes we make, from failing at a job or task, from personal traumas such as illness or divorce, and from being passed over for a promotion. Though rarely mentioned in any book or course on leadership, the important point is this: failure and suffering can propel us into the wilderness, encourage us to engage in deep introspection, and help us move beyond the shadow and toward our hidden wholeness. It is to this destination that we are beckoned.

The Gifts of the Inner Journey

Hidden wholeness is the first gift of the journey down and in. We feel better integrated, we spend less energy wearing masks and repressing or projecting the shadow, and the monsters are tamed (at least a bit). Claiming this gift doesn't mean that we won't ever again feel fragmented, or that other monsters won't appear, or that we no longer have a shadow. Life isn't like that. But now we know that there is a way through the wilderness, that we can ride the monsters all the way down and be better off for it. We aren't as afraid of encountering those monsters in the future. And as we complete this leg of the journey, we have a new reference point, a new sense of possibility for ourselves, a new perspective on our identities and our capacity to connect.

We receive other gifts related to the specific shadow we embrace. Earlier, I mentioned the five monsters that Palmer has found existing in the shadow. For each, he also identified a gift.

For the shadow of insecurity about identity, the "great spiritual gift that comes as one takes the inner journey is to know for certain that 'who I am' does not depend on 'what I do'. Identity does not depend on titles, or degrees, or functioning" (1998b, p. 205).

The spiritual gift we receive for embracing the belief hidden deep within that the "universe is essentially hostile to human interests" is the "knowledge that the universe is working together for good" (1998b, p. 13).

The gift we receive on the inner journey toward the shadow of functional atheism is the "certain knowledge that ours is not the only game in town . . . on this journey we learn that we do not have to carry the whole load, that we can be empowered by sharing our load with others, and that sometimes we can even lay part of our load down" (1998b, p. 206). Accepting this gift helps us in our move toward partnerships.

The fourth monster that Palmer identifies is the "fear of the natural chaos of life." The spiritual gift on the inner journey is to know that creation comes out of chaos. Accepting this gift helps us enjoy the turbulence of white water, to appreciate the energy and creativity we find in it, rather than longing for smooth waters.

The denial of death is the final shadow Palmer identifies. He suggests that the "spiritual gift on the inner journey is the gift of knowing that death is natural and that death is not the final word. The spiritual gift is to know that allowing something to die is allowing new life to emerge" (1998b, pp. 15, 16).

There is a gift beyond every shadow, a gift that is ours, but a gift that we receive only if we take the journey.

There are also more gifts that come from the journey that are not related to a particular monster. One of them is that our functioning at work is enhanced by the journey. We are more centered internally and better connected relationally. We work with more consciousness and creativity, more vitality and life. Energy once spent repressing the shadow is now freed for more productive and meaningful pursuits.

Another gift is a new kind of self-confidence—not confidence built on position power or status conferred by the corporation, but the confidence that comes when we embrace our total selves, our strengths and our limitations, our light and our shadow, and learn that we are OK as we are. It is self-confidence built on deep inner strength, the confidence we gain anytime we leave bondage and survive the wilderness.

Taking the inner journey also leads us to a sharper understanding and acceptance of our personal power. The individual who is truly empowered is the one who has some understanding of her or his shadow and develops some inner consciousness.

A fourth gift the journey promises us is that we will be better able to engage in the activity of leadership. The more awareness we have of our inner lives, the less tenuous and the more confident our involvement in leadership activities is.

A final gift we receive from the journey is the gift of genuine partnership (or, if you wish, real connectedness) in relationships. We become more understanding and accepting of others and better able to honor diversity; we have stronger and more meaningful relationships as a result of our personal and inner journeys. In the final analysis, it is the inner journey that we each must take that makes the whole notion of partnership-as-leadership possible.

Being and Doing

In this chapter and the preceding one, I have focused on aspects of identity, of being. I have argued that we must know ourselves (our whole self) and be ourselves before we can effectively engage in partnership. But there are also some things we can and must do to make new understandings and practices of leadership viable. Focusing on being to the exclusion of doing can degenerate into insipid navel-gazing. But doing without being lacks depth and authenticity. It is an empty exercise that is more dispiriting that inspiring. In the next chapters, the focus shifts from being to doing; however, it is done with a reminder that what's really important is being *and* doing.

Chapter Seven

What Are We to Do?

We serve when we build capability in others by
supporting ownership and choice at every level.
—*Peter Block (1993, p. 44)*

The primary question is one of choice. It is a question, or several questions, we each must ask: Am I being the kind of self I want to be? Am I creating the kind of relationships and work communities I want to live and work in? Am I building capability within myself and others that supports and encourages partnerships? Am I satisfied with how I have been involved in various leadership activities in these relationships and communities? If not, what must I do differently?

It is not enough to throw off the yoke of old leadership practices. We must be clear about what we can and will do to understand and practice leadership in new ways. It is an old saw, but true: with freedom comes responsibility, and partnership requires that each of us be responsible for acting anew.

It is not just executives who must change, though the obligation includes them. Each of us must develop capacities needed to do partnership-as-leadership. The first part of this chapter reviews ways that all of us can and must choose to act; later I examine the specific things that leaders (executives and managers) and followers must each choose to do differently if partnership-as-leadership is to work, if leadership and spirit are to be linked. Some of these ideas have been discussed at least in part in other sections of this book; I include them here for the sake of emphasis, and to link them more clearly to partnerships.

What Each of Us Must Do

For partnership-as-leadership to work, there are four specific things that each of us must do.

Claim Personal Power

In short, *we must claim our personal power*. For partnership-as-leadership to work, we must each claim the personal power that is within us. No more longing for sources of coercive power. Coercive power is a liability rather than an asset as we move to a new practice of leadership. By definition, coercive power creates winners and losers; builds one-up, one-down relationships; and encourages fear or dependency, none of which are helpful in partnerships.

No more waiting to be empowered, waiting for someone to share power with us, or give us power. Waiting to be empowered is like waiting for Santa Claus to come. We want someone else to give us a gift we don't think we have or don't think we can get on our own.

One of the choices we must make is to claim our personal power, the power that is based on belief in our self-worth, knowledge of our competence and expertise, and use of our native talents or gifts. This kind of power comes from within. It is not power over; it is "power to": the power to influence people and have an impact on events. This kind of power cannot be given to us or taken away from us; it is internal to us.

The use of coercive power engenders hostility and distrust in relationships. The use of personal power creates trust and openness. The former undercuts partnerships; the latter helps build them. As we claim and use our personal power

• We speak and act on the truth that is inside us. We find our voice and use it. There is no more saying yes when we want to say no; no more remaining silent when the group is making a decision we know will take us in a wrong direction; no more agreeing with the boss in the public meeting only to openly criticize him during the coffee break. There is less collusive behavior of any kind. Collusive behavior undermines partnerships, stifles creativity, hampers productivity, and suffocates spirit.

- We no longer accept responsibility for the thoughts and feelings of others, and we don't blame others for our internal realities. Blaming others for our thoughts, feelings, and behaviors gives away our power; it says someone else is responsible and we are not. So, no more "you made me angry" or "the devil made me do it"; rather, "I am angry" and "I did it and I am sorry." Even though it is not always true, it is better for me to act as if I were 100 percent responsible for my own thoughts, feelings, and behavior.

- We become more proactive, less reactive. No more sitting on the sidelines waiting for someone else to send us into the game. We don't wait for others to structure our work, give us direction, hand down a decision. We choose to be involved in activities of leadership.

- We expect to be treated as a partner, and we act as a partner. Not one-up or one-down, but straight across. We search for common ground, and look for the win for everyone involved. We learn from experience that I-thou relationships are more satisfying and ultimately more productive than I-it, collaboration is more effective than competition, and community is more meaningful than hierarchy.

- We act responsibly and are accountable even if we don't have authority. No more "change has to start at the top" or "they won't let us do it."

Claiming and using personal power is not easy to do, and it is harder for some people than others. There are situations and relationships in which it is easier, others in which it is harder. But we can and must learn to use our personal power effectively if partnership-as-leadership is to work. If we do it, we uncover and unleash the force called spirit. We are enlivened and energized, and we experience a breath of new life.

Honor Diversity

A second thing each of us must do is honor diversity. There are four affirmations essential to honoring diversity and linking it to partnerships:

- Every individual has a native gift or talent.
- Gifts differ. Every individual has a gift, but these gifts are not the same.
- These gifts can be used to enhance the activity of leadership.
- Partnership-as-leadership requires expression of these gifts.

The word *diversity* is often used in organizations in reference to racial, gender, religious, or ethnic differences. Although I acknowledge the deep importance of understanding and appreciating this understanding of diversity (including its importance to partnerships), I want to attach to the concept another meaning. I hope the concept I offer extends the more usual understandings of diversity by suggesting that all persons have gifts to offer in service to their work, and by suggesting that partnership-as-leadership works only when, as John Gardner suggested, we experience "wholeness incorporating diversity."

The concept of diversity of gifts is critical to the concept of identity. To honor a person requires honoring the native talent or gift that is part of that person's core identity. This doesn't always happen in the places where we work. Roles are not always assigned and boxes on the organization chart filled in consideration of the gifts of individuals. We draw tight boundaries around the roles—while calling it role clarification—to make sure individuals know what skills they can use and what gifts are not welcomed. Executives-as-leaders (and midlevel-managers-as-leaders) allocate resources, delegate work, and make assignments to important task forces based on position or place in hierarchy, rather than considering the gifts of individuals or the diversity of gifts reflected in the collective. As a result, we regularly put square pegs in round holes. Or we ask people to be less and to offer less than their best. Or we use the gifts of only a few. The gifts of the many are left unopened.

Even job-placement decisions are sometimes made that take people away from using their gifts, and only later does the organization learn the expensive lesson that not everyone wants an opportunity to go against the grain and develop new skills and capacities. Several years ago, I worked in an organization where research scientists were told that they couldn't stay on the bench but had to move into management ranks because the company wanted to be more scientifically driven in the future. As you might expect, several resisted; they wanted the company to acknowledge that gifts differ, to honor and use the gifts they had, and not to expect that everyone wanted to be a manager.

Gifts do differ. One person is intuitive, and another is better at analyzing quantitative data. One is conceptual, better at a long-range look at the future; another is detailed-oriented, better at organizing the present. One worker is effective at building multiple relationships across an entire organization; another is better at working alone or with a select group. One is a gifted writer who fears speaking in public; another is a talented presenter, at ease in front of even very large groups. One is artistic, another more mechanical. The differences seem so simple and so obvious, yet we don't always acknowledge them. Too often we expect others to be like us, think like us, act like us. Too often we do not acknowledge, much less celebrate, the wonderful richness that our unique gifts offer to the activity of leadership.

Every person—exempt or nonexempt, line or staff, management or worker—has a gift that can be used to enhance the activity of leadership. Regardless of level or function or age or experience, every individual has a gift that adds breadth and depth to partnerships. More than ever before, organizations need the creativity and energy that comes when individuals use their gifts in leadership activities. In fact, partnership-as-leadership *requires* that the diverse gifts of individuals be used. It is not an option. The partnership model is a collective model, one based on the premise that leadership is strengthened when all individuals express their special gifts. We each have a gift to offer and we each must offer that gift for partnership-as-leadership to work.

Consider these payoffs to honoring and using the gifts of all individuals:

• Doing so frees any one individual, even an executive or manager, from think or feeling that he or she must do it all. Most of us know something of our limitations. We know we don't have all the answers. We know that we are not as creative, or perhaps not as good at thinking systemically, or maybe not as good at building networks, as others are, and yet we think that we must be all and do all. We try to carry the entire burden because that's what expected of us, that's what we're paid the big bucks to do. If we honor the diversity of gifts of individuals, then no one person has to speak or act on behalf of all. One person does not have to be the leader and alone carry the mantle of responsibility and accountability. One person does not have to get to the point where he or she is simply used up.

• It helps each of us to know that we are needed, that we do have something special to offer to the practice of leadership in the organization in which we spend so much of our time. As we experience making our unique contribution, we are inspired. We find new energy and vitality. Using our gifts is a spiritual act.

• It makes our work communities stronger. Diversity, when honored, always does this. It doesn't necessarily make things easier, or more efficient, but it does make leadership more effective and organizations stronger. This is especially true when, over time, we build trust and a sense of connectedness and learn effective ways of working together.

Learn New Skills

A third thing we must each do is learn new skills. There are specific relationship skills that we can and must learn if we are to implement a practice of leadership that is inspiriting. There are four skills that I consider essential. The first two—deep listening and speaking for oneself—are basic and may seem elementary, but I have found that they are hard to integrate into day-to-day behavior. The second two—dialogue and conflict holding—are more sophisticated and perhaps even harder to use effectively.

Deep Listening. The first skill we must learn and integrate is the skill of deep listening. When I was starting my career in training and development, I spent several years leading courses developed by Thomas Gordon, president of Effectiveness Training Associates. The most popular of these courses was Parent Effectiveness Training (PET), but the one I enjoyed leading the most was Leader Effectiveness Training. LET was carefully designed to teach managers and executives the interpersonal skills they needed to build and maintain important work relationships. The foundation skill, on which all other interpersonal skills were built, was listening.

One of the most important things I learned from working with many managers from all levels of organizations is that we need to unlearn old habits while learning new ones. We need to unlearn the habit of doing two things at once, of attempting to listen while thumbing through papers on our desk or finishing a paragraph on a report we are writing. Our mind wanders to what else we need to do, or we start focusing on how we will respond. The first key to listening is simply this: be present.

The second key to listening is to pay attention. Giving another person your undivided attention, if only for a few minutes, honors that person. It communicates that he or she is important. It encourages the person to express the deepest of longings or fears. It liberates spirit.

Recently, I was in an airport waiting for a flight that had been delayed, when I bumped into a colleague. Our conversation wasn't deep, but still I was struck by his ability to pay attention. I was distracted by the noises and people around us, and I was keeping one eye on the counter to see if there was any news about the flight. But he paid attention to me and to what I was saying. It had an impact.

I experienced his presence with me. Paying attention during conversations in a hectic space is something we can learn to do.

Another old habit we must unlearn for better listening is interrupting to send the other person a solution before he or she has had time to explain the problem, or to let us know what is really wanted or needed. We are so problem-focused, and our jobs so often require that we solve problems and that we solve them quickly, that we leap into problem-solving mode even when dealing with people. The problem-solving skills that are strengths as we work on technical problems turn into liabilities in working with people. Most often, what people want is to be heard, to have an opportunity to express what they are thinking and feeling, to get something off their chest. What they don't want or need is for us to jump in quickly and attempt to solve their problem for them.

Be present. Pay attention. Hold your tongue. These relatively simple things go a long way in encouraging better flow of thoughts and feelings. But there are positive things we can do as well: we can learn to ask open-ended questions (questions that are not statements in disguise; questions for which we don't already know the answer); we can learn to paraphrase and ask clarifying questions; we can learn to hear beyond the words another person uses so that we can "hear" their thoughts and feelings; and we can learn effective ways of checking out what we've heard to see if we've gotten the message.

As we learn to listen deeply, we also learn how to allow others to own the problems that belong to them. If we solve problems for others—especially those problems that are internal to them—we take away their personal power, and we assume responsibility for those problems.

Learning the skills of deep listening also helps us show empathy. Simply defined, empathy is feeling *with* another person; in contrast, sympathy is feeling *for* them. Carl Rogers defined empathy as one of the three characteristics of a helping relationship. It moves us in concrete ways toward an I-thou relationship.

Speaking for Ourselves. The second skill we must learn is to speak for ourselves. To paraphrase a book title of several years ago, we must listen in such a way that others will speak, and we must speak such that others will listen.

In the preceding chapter, I talked about the importance of being authentic. I also suggested that how we express ourselves, how we speak our truth and express our thoughts and feelings, is important. In short, we must learn to speak for self.

It is easier and less risky to speak for others. "We think you could be more effective if. . . ." "The president wanted me to tell you. . . ." "They said we had to. . . ." "The group talked about it and they wanted me to tell you." It is harder to speak for self: "I felt good when you said you would leave time to hear from each of us, but then I was disappointed when there was so much you had to communicate that there wasn't really time to hear from us." "I think we are 'going to Abilene'. Before we go further, I would like to check in and make sure we are in agreement about this decision." "I was upset when you came into the meeting and took over the agenda." "I felt valued and appreciated when you included me in that decision."

Speaking for self is a way of claiming our personal power. If I say "You upset me" or "You made me angry," I'm suggesting that *you* are in charge of my feelings, and I am not. "I am upset" or "I am grateful" communicates that *I* own the feelings, that I am responsible for them and you are not.

Deftly done, speaking for ourselves allows us to express our truths without blaming something or someone else. Thus, I lessen the possibility that I will tear at the fabric of our relationship or that what I say will provoke a defensive response. It offers a way to be authentic without being dispiriting.

Speaking for self is a characteristic of partnerships. Skip LeFauvre is a senior vice president at General Motors; formerly he was chairman and president of Saturn Corporation, a company he helped launch. LeFauvre recently wrote that the greatest management achievement at Saturn was to develop a consensus to what their approach should be. LeFauvre acknowledged that in an organization the size of Saturn not every member of the leadership team could always be 100 percent supportive of every decision, but he argued that every individual had to be comfortable enough with the action to be able to say "we made the decision" rather than "they decided." "They decided" is speaking for others; "we decided" is speaking for self. If leadership is understood and practiced as partnership, we are able to honestly speak for ourselves.

There is a danger in thinking of deep listening and speaking for self as just another set of skills and reducing them to technique. Listening that is not based on truly caring about the other person and what he or she is feeling and thinking is just technique—clever but not genuine, and usually not helpful. Speaking for self without knowing and owning our inner drives and motives—without knowing ourselves—is not an authentic expression. Being and doing are interwoven, and knowing ourselves is a must if we are to effectively use these interpersonal communication skills.

Deep listening and speaking for self, as I suggested, are the primary skills; they are needed to build and maintain any relationship, including partnership-as-leadership. The other two skills needed to implement partnerships—dialogue and holding conflict—are built on these primary skills.

Dialogue. The third skill is dialogue. *Dialogue* is an old word that in recent years has taken on new meaning. It is not the same as conversation, discussion, or debate. In a discussion, and usually in a debate, contrasting views are often presented and defended, and one idea tends to prevail over others. But dialogue, Peter Senge reminds us, is different: "Dialogue is the capacity of members to suspend assumptions and enter into a genuine thinking together. To the Greek, 'dia-logos' meant a free-flowing of meaning through a group, allowing the group to attain insights not available individually" (1990, pp. 10, 247).

In dialogue, multiple views are presented as a way of discovering yet another view. This essential characteristic of dialogue—

a free flowing of meaning among partners that leads to insights not available to individuals—is what makes partnership-as-leadership work. It is through the experience of dialogue that new truths are discovered, that meaning is made, that true partnerships emerge.

Dialogue is based on the premise that there is meaning outside any particular individual, and that this meaning is accessible if, for example, partners in the activity of leadership suspend their assumptions and "think together." In dialogue, individuals don't come together with objective truth in hand, ready to impose that truth on others; instead, they gather with a commitment to search for another truth or a new truth not already known or obvious.

Contrast this with how, typically, we believe we know truth in the organizations in which we work. In *The Courage to Teach* (1998a), Parker Palmer suggests that the dominant model for knowing the truth is based on four assumptions: (1) that truth is objective and can be known by comprehending facts; (2) that experts are the people who have these facts; (3) that amateurs are the people who need to be taught the facts; and (4) that baffles exist at every point in the transmission to ensure that objective truth flows down and that no subjective opinions flow back up. Palmer applied this model to the educational process; it applies equally well to hierarchical business organizations in which executive-as-leader is in vogue. The executives are assumed to be the experts, truth flows from them, and baffles interrupt the flow of information back up the organizational ladder. Truth, it is assumed, is possessed by individuals called leaders, rather than being found within the partnership.

David Bohm has identified three conditions necessary for dialogue to happen; all three relate specifically to partnership-as-leadership. First, assumptions must be suspended. Suspending assumptions does not mean denying them, ignoring them, or pretending they don't exist. Suspending assumptions means that we know, and are willing to hold in front of ourselves, our assumptions of how things ought be, what ideas are right, what decision should be made, so that our preconceived notions don't block the free flow of information.

The second precondition of dialogue is that all participants in the dialogue must regard each other as colleagues. Bohm argued that hierarchy was antithetical to dialogue. This is true even if the person at the top of the hierarchy wishes it to be different. For dialogue to work, managers and executives must want dialogue more than they want command and control, and those we now call subordinates (but whom we ought call partners) must risk being authentic and expressing what they honestly think and feel. In our understanding and in our relationships, we must switch from boss-subordinate relationships to partnerships. The switch has to be more than a word game, more than putting new wine in old wineskins. It is this simple: for partnership-as-leadership to happen, there must be dialogue, and for dialogue to happen, we must see one another as colleagues and partners.

One of the ways we learn to engage in dialogue is through what Bohm identified as the third precondition: using a skilled facilitator. The facilitator keeps the idea flowing, makes sure assumptions are surfaced and suspended, and encourages individuals to act as colleagues. It is best that this facilitator be a disinterested person, someone who is not part of the work community and who has no stake in a particular outcome, but who can focus on process.

Holding Conflict. Another skill we need to learn for partnerships to work is conflict holding. Holding conflict means allowing it to be. It means putting differences on the table and allowing them to stay there, with no rushing to manage or resolve them. This is not what we usually do.

We tend to think of conflict as a bad thing. We think that a relationship is in trouble or a team is not functioning well if there is evidence of conflict. Often our fears are well founded. We all have had the experience of conflict tearing at the fabric of a relationship. We have participated in meetings that disintegrated because two people disagreed. We have seen partnerships come apart at the seams because differences could not be managed.

We also fear conflict because throughout our lives it has been resolved in a win-lose way. One person demands; the other flinches and accommodates. One idea prevails, and another is diminished. One individual or group gets its needs met; the other does not. We've experienced conflict as a win-lose proposition in relationships with parents, teachers, and bosses.

Because of these formative experiences, most of us avoid conflict whenever we can. One of the ways we avoid conflict is by not speaking our truth. We stay quiet even if we know there is real but unsurfaced disagreement in the group about a decision being made, but we fear creating conflict and not being seen as a team player more than we fear a poor decision.

The temptation to remain quiet happens even in senior-level management teams. One executive team I have worked with appeared very harmonious when they were together. In public meetings no one sounded a discordant note. Conflict stayed beneath the surface. But if disagreements and conflict did surface, they came out sideways—in conversations with a third party such as an HR professional or a consultant, or in lobbying for a particular decision with the president after a meeting was over.

We also stay quiet when we know the other person has power over us, and we are afraid of that person or dependent on him or her. The greater the perceived or real power differential in a relationship, the greater the possibility we will hold our tongue and keep conflicts beneath the surface. In the executive-as-leader model, it is usually the executive who has power, and it is the rest of us who don't speak our truths.

If staying quiet is no longer possible, we try to resolve the conflict as quickly as possible. We attempt to smooth over it, to pour oil on troubled waters. Or we deny our needs and accommodate those of the other, so that the conflict will disappear. Thus we lose and the other wins, but we think this is OK because the conflict has dissipated. Or we see conflict surfacing and decide to do whatever is necessary to prevail, using whatever coercive power we have at our disposal. We threaten, cajole, promise, pressure—whatever it takes to win. The goal, of course, is to make the conflict disappear.

It seems strange, then, to consider holding conflict. Not avoiding it, not trying to manage or resolve it as quickly as possible, but actually acknowledging it and holding it in front of us.

Holding conflict requires, first of all, that we believe that conflict can be a positive sign. In any partnership, if two or more people who share power speak and act on their truths, there are going to be disagreements and conflict. It is bound to happen. Rather than see expression of differences as a negative, we can begin to understand that the presence of conflict means that each person in the partnership is speaking his or her truth, trying to get needs met, and attempting to have influence and impact.

Let me share an example. Several years ago, I worked for eighteen months as a volunteer facilitator for a sixty-person citizen group charged with the responsibility of developing a school redistricting plan, a plan for assigning students to schools in a way that would make best use of facilities, minimize transportation costs, and ensure racial and economic diversity. Each of the task force members represented a neighborhood or community group. Each had a specific agenda to accomplish in addition to the shared goal of "doing what's best for the children." No one had power over anyone else. In this setting, conflict was inevitable. But in this committee, as in so many other relationships, the tendency at first was to keep the conflict under the table, or to manage it quickly ("let's take a vote") if it surfaced. It was hard for members of the committee—much less people in the community who were not on the committee—to see the conflicts, the real differences, as a positive. Even the local newspapers tended to report the conflicts as chaotic and to suggest that the committee was disintegrating. But the conflicts surfaced and were often positive—not easy or enjoyable, not always productive. But sometimes they were. The conflicts meant that each person was giving voice to deeply held concerns and beliefs. They meant that no decision was going to be made simply because one person or group accommodated. It also meant that not every decision would be completely shared; this simply wasn't possible in a group that size. In the process of learning to hold the conflicts, the group became stronger.

As we hold conflict, we examine what it has to teach us. We try to discover the truth that the conflict is communicating to us. Anytime conflict is held, we have the opportunity, as we do in dialogue, to discover truths that are not available to us individually. Understood in this way, holding conflict is a critical skill needed in implementing partnerships.

Claiming our personal power, honoring diversity, developing new skills . . . these are things that each of us must do if we are to implement a new practice of leadership. But there are also particular things that executives and managers (formerly the leaders) and followers must do to implement partnership-as-leadership.

What Executives Must Do

So, what's an executive (or manager) to do?

If the understanding and practice of leadership centered on the individual-as-leader does not evoke spirit, does not elicit the best that others have within them, then what's an executive or manager to do to help the organization accomplish its mission and goals?

If it is not the executive's role to be *the* leader, if it is not his or her role to create a vision and articulate it compellingly, what is he or she to do?

If leadership is more process-centered than person-centered, what's the role of the person who occupies the corner office on the top floor or the only office on the shop floor?

(In a way, the distinction between executives and followers— the distinction made in this section and the next—is artificial, and thus not helpful. For partnerships to work effectively, we must all do everything described in each section. But partnership-as-leadership has not been used in most organizations; most still have leaders and followers. I make the distinction, then, because there are things that executives and followers must do differently if they are to move toward a new understanding and practice of leadership.)

Tend to the Process

The first thing an executive or manager must do is tend to the process. The practice of partnership requires creating new processes—individual, interpersonal, and organizational. Creating and convening these processes, and tending to their use, can be an important role for the manager or executive.

If an executive or manager believes that because of position or status, experience or expertise, he or she possesses truth that must be shared if not imposed, it will be hard to think of his or her role as convening and tending the process. But if an executive realizes that his or her role is to create a space where dialogue can happen, where truth can be discovered, and where day-to-day decisions can be made, he or she can then quit being *the* leader and start convening the process in which the activity of leadership happens.

This is an understandably hard shift for executives to make. They have experience and expertise that is important to the organization. They ride a higher helicopter, as I suggested earlier in this book, and thus have a longer-range perspective than others. They are used to exercising their power. They are accountable for organizational results. None of these perspectives and responsibilities can be discounted. To the contrary, each must be honored and effectively used. In partnership-as-leadership, an executive's experience and expertise, longer-range view, power, and sense of accountability are important to the effectiveness of the activity of leadership. The difference is that the executive is now doing *with* rather than *to*, is using personal power rather than coercive power, and shares responsibility and accountability so that partnerships can be created and optimum results can be attained.

An executive begins tending to the process as he or she tends to self—when she, with intention and attention, models being an authentic self (the kind of self that is important to partnerships), when she speaks truth without blame or judgment, when she abandons herself to the strengths of others. An executive who refuses to be compartmentalized and instead uses all her energies in her work, who risks being open and vulnerable even to the point of saying at times "I don't know," who chooses courage over collusion, who uses personal power rather than the power of her position, who embraces her shadow rather than projects it, is tending to the process. In sum, an executive can fully participate in the activity of leadership in a way that models a better way of being, and a new way of doing leadership.

On the interpersonal level, convening and tending the process means, first of all, bringing people together to work collaboratively toward accomplishing a shared goal. At times, and depending on the size of the organization or workgroup within a larger organization, it may mean bringing all people of the community together. Future Search Conferences, a technology developed by Marvin Weisbord and several of his colleagues, is a process that brings all stakeholders of an organization together to cocreate a shared understanding of their future. The conferences can involve hundreds of people in an act of cocreation. It amounts to actualizing partnerships in large groups.

At other times, it involves bringing smaller workgroups together. I know of one workgroup (inside an organization) of some twenty individuals who are working to develop an understanding and practice of leadership that allows all of them to be constituted as the leadership team. The director of the group understands his role as convening the process by bringing members of the team together. In this workgroup, a distinction is made between the management group (a smaller group of individuals) and the leadership team, which is all members of the work community.

At other times, convening the process may require gathering into a leadership team an important but short-term task force team to work on a critical business issue. Not every leadership team or work community has to be ongoing.

Finally, bringing people together may mean making sure that two individuals whose open differences are having negative consequences for the entire organization are brought together and given an opportunity to acknowledge and make sense of their differences, and decide if they want to hold and honor them, or work through them.

Anytime an executive brings people together and gives them a chance to act as partners, the executive is tending the process.

But there is often more to tending interpersonal processes than bringing people together. Tending the process is also encouraging dialogue. It is inviting disagreement and tough questions. It is making sure conflict is not ignored. It is involving partners in solving the ambiguous problems of the organization. It is paying attention to who is included and who isn't, to who feels free to speak their truth and who is not yet comfortable doing so, who uses personal power and participates with courage and who still says yes while wanting to say no, who knows and uses a gift and who is yet to discern it. Tending the process is honoring people wherever they are on the journey, while encouraging them to be all they can be. It is making sure that full participation in partnerships is available, while acknowledging that individuals have varying ability and willingness to engage fully.

On an organizational level, tending the process involves making sure that structures and systems support partnerships. Partnership-as-leadership requires more than developing new leadership capacities by individuals. It also requires development of supportive organizational structures, systems, and processes. To continue the metaphor of the tapestry, individual growth and development *and* organization development must be woven together if partnerships are to work effectively. They must also be woven together into a seamless tapestry. To fully implement partnerships, we must take this holistic approach to development.

In developing the organization, executives can facilitate the movement away from hierarchies toward more weblike organizations, where interdependencies are clear and the need for partnerships is evident. Freeing individuals from straight lines and boxes and putting them in interconnected circles—symbolically doing this in new organizational charts and literally doing it in organizing to accomplish the work of the organization—is a powerful and important step in developing partnership-as-leadership.

Executives can also work to make sure that organizational systems are in alignment, so that, for example, the performance-appraisal system reinforces work done collaboratively and the compensation system rewards work in partnerships (and, conversely, does not reward only strong heroic performance by individuals).

Participate Fully

Another thing executives must do is participate fully in the activity of leadership. There is a larger role for the executive than simply convening and tending to the process; he or she must be a full and active participant in it.

Like other participants in the activity of leadership, executives must deeply listen, speak for self as they tell their truths, engage in dialogue, and hold conflict. They must also exercise their personal power and have influence and impact on directions taken and decisions made. Creating a practice of leadership based on partnership does not mean that the executive abdicates role and responsibility. The executive must not give away power. Moving to collaboration is different from moving to accommodation. Collaboration—exercising the partnership model—does not mean allowing unacceptable directions to be taken or wrong decisions to be made. No direction or decision is a good one unless it meets the needs of the executive and the needs of the organization as the executive understands them.

Moving to collaboration also does not mean allowing decisions to languish. One executive I worked with was so intent on opening up the processes in the organization he headed, so determined that things should "bubble up," that important decisions got put off rather than made in a timely way. One role of the executive in tending to the process is to make sure that decisions get made.

Executives must use their knowledge, experience, and expertise to have an impact on all leadership activities, large and small, in which they are involved. The difference now is that the executives have moved from positional power to personal power, from command and control to collaboration; influence and impact is shared, and at times the executive even abandons self to the strengths of others.

Decline the Leader Role

A third thing executives must do is refuse to be *the* leader. Some followers expect and encourage an executive to be the leader; at other times, the executive feels he or she has earned it. As suggested earlier, some individuals appear not to want to be involved in the activity of leadership; they only want their dictator to be benevolent—a good father or mother. For these individuals, deferring to and deifying the leader is learned behavior. An unintended consequence of using a top-down, executive-as-leader model over time and reinforcing it with rewards and punishments is that some followers learn passivity and powerlessness. For other followers, involvement in the activity of leadership appears too risky. Being involved, having one's voice heard, and having influence mean becoming accountable. With freedom to participate in the activity of leadership comes responsibility, and there are some who choose to give up the former for fear of the latter. Whatever the reason, there are many individuals who would, if given the opportunity, be pleased to participate in the coronation of *the* leader. Though the temptation is great, the executive must refuse the throne if that is what is needed to ever get the full and complete energies of the men and women of the organization committed to accomplishing the mission.

Executives must find ways to satisfy their ego needs other than being *the* leader. It is my experience that this can be done if executives link their ego needs to the success of the organization rather than to their personal goals. In *Sacred Hoops*, Phil Jackson talked about what he did to coax Michael Jordan to do less so that the Chicago Bulls could do more. The coach knew that scoring champions rarely play for championship teams; it is too easy for playoff teams to tighten their defenses and prevent one great scorer from beating them. Jordan came to realize that for the Bulls to win another championship the offensive system had to be more important than his individual goals—including another scoring title. This is a tough transition for any individual to make, but one that is made easier if team goals replace individual goals as a source of ego gratification.

An executive or manager who chooses to move toward a new understanding and practice of leadership must realize that change of this magnitude—change in how things get done in the organization—requires time, patience, and willingness to move deliberately but slowly. Moving to a practice of leadership that engages all the energies of people, including their spiritual energy, is more akin to swinging the *Queen Mary* around than to turning around a car. There are times when progress is not evident. There are temptations to return to tried-and-true ways of leading. But if the executive stays the course, remembers the purpose, and is patient, then progress can and will be made. The result is worth it: a workforce with esprit de corps, with women and men fully engaged and fully committed to accomplishing the organization's mission.

What "Followers" Must Do

What about those individuals we have up to now called followers? What must they do differently if an understanding and practice of partnership-as-leadership is to be realized?

An important assumption underlying partnerships is that during the course of their careers most people must be involved in leadership activities in order to fulfill their commitment to the organization in which they work. In these leadership activities, the individual may at times have formal authority (being a group's representative on a committee), but just as likely they are involved in leadership activities where they have no formal authority but only their personal power as a resource (a team member who helps the workgroup focus on its core values and on the purpose of their work, as an example).

There are several important things that followers must do if they are to become full partners.

Choose Courage

First, they must choose courage over collusion. As pointed out in Chapter Three, collusion is one of the significant ways followers encourage what they say they don't want: command-and-control, top-down leadership. It is one of the primary reasons that this practice of leadership has continued.

Collusion comes in many guises. We disagree with the direction in which an executive is taking the organization, or a decision that has been made, and we complain about it over a luncheon conversation with friends, or in the hallway during a break in a meeting. But we say nothing to the executive. We even complain that no one is willing to tell the executive that people in the organization are not following where they are being led, but we refuse any suggestion that we might be the person to deliver the message; "after all," we say, "they shoot the messenger, don't they?"

Over the years, I have seen this dynamic play out time after time in the realistic leadership simulation named Looking Glass. One of the problems built into this simulation is "Deepsea," a code name of a project in one of the imaginary company's three divisions to develop an underwater glass that the U.S. Navy could use in submarines. There is no evidence that the division can build the glass to the Navy's specification, even after pouring millions of dollars into the development effort. There is also no commitment from the Navy to buy the glass if it is developed. Any reasonable analysis of the data suggests that it is time for Looking Glass to deep-six Deepsea. But it is seldom done. The reason: the simulation presents a memo suggesting that this is a pet project of the company president. No one wants to tell the emperor he has no clothes. Remember, this is a simulated company, one in which there is no real consequence if the messenger does get shot. The participants in the simulation are usually middle-to-senior-level managers and executives from Fortune 1000 companies. The simulation shows us that even seasoned and respected managers, not just those who are new or are faint of heart, engage in collusive behavior.

Another form of collusive behavior is known as groupthink. The dynamic is as understandable as it is simple: an individual in a meeting slowly begins to sense that the group supports a position different from his own. Because the individual wants to be seen as a supportive member of the community and not the odd man out, he doesn't share his position. He gives into peer pressure. He goes along to get along. Later, when the decision made by the group turns out not to work as well as anticipated, under his breath if not out loud he says, "I knew it." This is collusion.

In *Reframing Organizations* (1991), Lee Bolman and Terry Deal report that this is exactly what happened in the *Challenger* disaster. On the evening before the launch of the space shuttle, engineers at Morton Thiokol, the company that provided the now infamous O-rings, suggested that the launch not lift off as scheduled. The engineers had insufficient data about how the O-rings would function in the cold temperatures that were expected. But managers at both Thiokol and NASA felt pressure to proceed with a liftoff, and Thiokol engineers finally relented. They said yes after first saying no, and they said yes when they still wanted to say no. This is collusion.

We are given opportunities to participate in an activity of leadership—from helping to write a new mission statement to being involved in mundane activities such as deciding to develop a more responsive infrastructure—and we decline. Our plate is already too full, we say. Sometimes it is. But sometimes we'd rather stay on the sidelines and lob verbal hand grenades than get involved in messy and complex leadership processes. Several years ago, a direct report complained to me that the basic compensation practice of our organization was unfair. Her argument was simple, that a 4 percent merit increase meant that those making $50,000 would be getting a significantly higher actual increase than those making $20,000, and that, over time, the disparity would continue to widen. Her argument, I thought, had merit. We were a small group at the time, and I invited all members of that work community to join with me in making sense out of an admittedly sensitive and complex topic. They refused. Their response was best characterized by a member of the community who said, "You get paid the big bucks and sit in the corner office to figure out things like this." This is collusion, not simply because of the unwillingness to participate, but because complaints about the merit system continued.

Choosing courage over collusion is hard to do. It runs counter to how we grew up around authority figures ("Children are to be seen not heard"); we weren't encouraged to find our voices and speak our truths. Few parents or teachers or other significant adults thought in terms of partnership. Few bosses do today. Choosing courage over collusion involves risk, a risk that is real and must be measured. Over time, we must become aware and accepting of our dependency needs and our fears, slowly let go of our fears as we practice speaking our truth, be willing to live with some awkward moments, and be intentional about avoiding collusive behavior.

Be Present

A second thing followers must do is be present and stay engaged in the tough work of the work community. For partnership-as-leadership to work, we must each decide to stay engaged in the all aspects of work in the organization.

It is fairly easy to think of creating a vision statement as something that happens in a collective, and to stay engaged in the process. A work community goes away for a retreat, and through a carefully guided process members develop a vision that captures a shared sense of what it means for the community to achieve greatness. It is also relatively easy to be present and stay engaged in developing a collective understanding of core values, or a shared sense of organizational mission. Most of us want to be involved in these activities. These leadership activities provide times for us to describe our own hopes about a preferred future for the work community, and the environment in which this important work is done is usually low-risk and safe.

It is harder to be present and stay engaged in the nitty-gritty of community life. Over time, I have learned that budgets drive organizational strategies as much as strategies drive budgets (if not more so). The strategies of an organization can often be determined better by taking a retrospective look at where money was spent in the past fiscal year than by looking at the strategy statement for the future. But preparing and negotiating budgets is not as much fun as creating vision statements. Most of us would prefer not to get our fingernails dirty digging into and making meaning out of income and expense. But this is where much organizational meaning is made, and so this is where each of us must be present and stay engaged if partnership is to be more than a nice phrase.

There are many other leadership activities in which we might choose not to be involved. Here are some instances.

• Two competing groups within a department have conflicting strategies for how the department ought best accomplish its business objectives. There are pros and cons to both strategies. Neither seems clearly superior. Trying to talk about it quickly brings differences to the surface. It is easier to let "them" decide, or to let the conflict stay hidden.

• Lately, your work community has been struggling with a complex and ambiguous problem of future direction, a problem for which there are no easy answers. New competitors have entered the business and are offering similar products at lower cost. Their products have not been as rigorously designed and are not as well tested or as reliable, and you know that you cannot recover your development costs if you lower your price to meet the competition. Plus, your organization has strong norms around maintaining quality. Your market share is slowly eroding. What to do? Let "them" decide.

• Your organization decided to move to self-managed work-teams. At first, while you were setting norms and expectations, clarifying mission and values, it was exciting. But now issues are getting sticky. It is time for performance to be appraised, and one teammate's work is unacceptable and he needs to be disciplined. But these activities can get tense, even conflictual, and you'd prefer not to be involved.

It is situations like these in which each of us must be present and stay engaged if partnership-as-leadership is to work. Being present, staying involved, learning and using new skills like dialogue and conflict holding, exercising our personal power . . . all of these are important to partnerships, and all are hard to do. We must realize that we haven't had many opportunities to practice and learn these unaccustomed leadership behaviors, that we are low on the learning curve. We must be patient with ourselves and others as we learn, and we must be willing to learn from our mistakes, give others freedom to make mistakes, live through and with the awkwardness that always accompanies development of new ways of doing, and consciously decide to stick with it until the new behaviors are somewhat integrated and feel more natural. This is the only way we develop the skills we need to make partnerships work.

Avoid "Crowning" Bosses

The fourth thing followers must do is not engage in the "coronation" of bosses. Executives and managers deserve our respect, not our reverence; our attention and appreciation, but not our adulation; our commitment, not a coronation.

Coronations and collusive behavior are linked. After the coronation of an executive, we work hard to please, even to the extent of giving up our identity, our sense of self, in order to do so. Giving up identity to please someone else is the definition of codependent behavior.

Coronations are heady stuff. The ego gratification of ruling over a "kingdom," if even for a day, would be hard for any of us to resist. So it is not unusual for executives to be seduced by the attraction of having the power, prestige, and status that accompany a coronation.

But it is not what bosses need—and often not even what they really want. Executives need colleagues who act interdependently rather than codependently. They need men and women working with them who act on and give voice to their truths. They need others who share responsibility and accountability. They need individuals who give the best that is within them to help accomplish the mission of the organization. They need partners, not subordinates.

It is a question of choice. The choice we each must make is between dependency and partnership. One leads toward executive-as-leader. The other leads toward partnership-as-leadership.

Chapter Eight

Fostering Community

We hunger for community and are a great deal
more productive when we find it.
                    —*Marvin Weisbord (1991, p. xiv)*

[We have] a deep desire for autonomy and self-
reliance combined with an equally deep conviction
that life has no meaning unless shared with others
in the context of community.
                    —*Robert Bellah (1985, p. 150)*

It wasn't that long ago that most business organizations existed as
pure hierarchies. They were considered the best way of organizing to
get work done efficiently and productively. Usually they worked. In
times when goals and objectives could be set and followed because
there was stability in the external and internal environment, hierarchies worked. When clear lines of authority and accountability were
more important than collaboration and commitment, hierarchies
worked. But even when they worked, hierarchies suggested a need
for few leaders and many workers.

The Reemergence of Community

But in recent times the advent of the knowledge worker and the
changing expectations of all workers, the rapid spread of new technology, and the slow dawning that we do in fact live in a time of permanent white water—in which organizations need the commitment

and creativity and energy of all workers—has led to new interest in better ways of organizing. One possibility is the idea of community. It suggests that all workers can and must be involved in the activity of leadership.

In a recent article, Gifford Pinchot suggested that today "few organizations exist as pure hierarchies or pure communities . . . but in the Information Age, the rapid spread of knowledge and the heightened needs of cooperation are bringing community to the forefront" (1998, p. 41). We must foster community and continue to bring it to the forefront if partnership-as-leadership is to work. Partnerships require strong individuals and a strong sense of connectedness. Partnerships require that we know ourselves and be willing to fully use the self; they also require that we foster and fully use community. It cannot be either-or; it must be both-and.

The definition of leadership offered in this book—two or more people sharing power and working interdependently toward a shared goal—is based on the importance of this both-and. The basic premise of partnerships is that leadership happens in a collective, that it emerges from the reciprocity of relationships, and that in the collective—whether it is a two-person relationship, a team, or a larger work community—individuals must be honored or else true leadership does not emerge. Simply put, we cannot have partnerships unless we weave together the individual and the community.

Though it is now coming to the forefront, the concept of community is not a new reality. It is reemerging. In "Building Corporations as Communities," Juanita Brown and David Issacs remind us that "for millennia, communities have been the most powerful mechanisms for creating human cooperation and reliable interdependence. By contrast, corporations and large-scale organizations have been a powerful force for the last hundred years or so . . . industrial enterprises have improved living standards for many millions of people. . . . [But] in the process, millions of us have been cut off from our yearning to be part of a larger community of endeavor that is worthy of our best effort" (1995, p. 69). In acknowledging the importance of community, we are once again making our old story our new story.

The Individual and Community

The last three chapters focused on being and doing, on who we must *be* and what we must *do* for leadership and spirit to be woven together in the understanding and practice of leadership that we've called partnership. The emphasis was on individual being and doing.

This is an important part of the story. Spirit works within us; it is the unseen force that defines the self that each of us brings to partnerships. We cannot be effective in partnerships without knowing and fully using that self. It is an important part of the story; but it is only a part.

Spirit also works among us to foster connectedness and community. The quote from George Leonard in Chapter Two says it clearly: what he calls silent pulse I call spirit, and thanks to it we "are completely, firmly, absolutely connected with all of existence." Each of us is connected in some way to everything else.

We want to individuate, to be the true and best self we can be. This is one of our core purposes as we grow, develop, and mature. We also want to belong to, be part of, and experience deep connectedness. This is another of our core purposes, and a source of deep meaning and satisfaction. We want to be independent, be able to stand on our own two feet, to make our own decisions. The ability to do each of these things is important to our identity. We also "hunger for community," the opening quote from Weisbord says; we make sense of our lives through relationships and community. This need for community is critical to our understanding of the self that we bring to activities of leadership.

There is tension, at least at times, between our need to be apart from and our need to be a part of, a tension between our need to individuate and our need for community. We fear that we will have to give up our sense of self if we are going to be part of community, that we will lose our identity to that of the group. This can and does happen; individuals sometimes get swallowed up by groups. The reverse is also true. We also know from experience that our desire to be ourselves and the urgency we feel to protect the self keep us from finding the connectedness and community we want and for which we hunger. The tension between the need to be individuals and our need to belong is real and appears inevitable. Our task is not to resolve this tension, but rather to be ourselves *and* experience community in the midst of the tension.

In the United States, this tension is not always kept in balance. We love the Lone Ranger, literally and symbolically, and still hope that there is a masked man with silver bullets out there who can rescue us from life's perils and pitfalls. We still look for heroic leaders to bestow on us safety and security. We shy away from too much connectedness and community in order to protect ourselves. We want to be cowboys more than we want community, or at least we want to be seen this way.

A friend and colleague, Michael Hoppe, is a student of cross-cultural perspectives on leadership. In a recent publication, *The Center for Creative Leadership Handbook of Leadership Development*, he reports that across many studies Americans are shown to be highly individualistic, especially when compared to individuals from other countries. We tend to see leadership as an individual phenomenon rather than something that emerges from a group or community, and we tend to protect and act on our need to be individuals more than we act on our need for community.

Practicing partnerships helps us find some balance between our need to be ourselves and our need to belong. Engaging in partnerships encourages us to be ourselves; it also encourages us to act collaboratively. Engaging in partnerships frees us to use all of our personal power, no holding back; and it encourages others to use their power (not power that we give to them, remember, but power they already have). Partnerships require that we use our gifts, skills, and energies; as we engage in partnerships we learn to do so. But partnerships also require that we honor the diversity of gifts and skills that others bring to the activity of leadership; in doing partnership-as-leadership, we learn this as well.

There is one more important link. Practicing partnerships fosters development of community, and the presence of community makes this practice of leadership more possible. Partnerships and community are linked. Spirit is also linked here because it works among us to foster a sense of connectedness. Our spirituality is developed, in part, by the practice of partnership and in the experience of community. In this way, leadership, spirit, and community are interwoven.

The Importance of Community

The importance of individual and community to the practice of partnerships is just one of the reasons that we must foster community. There are other reasons community is important, all related to partnerships. Let's turn our attention to three of them.

Community as Metaphor

Community is an important metaphor for our places of work. Remember Composite Corporation from the opening of this book? At one time the people of Composite used the metaphor of family to describe their company, but no more. Composite grew too large and too impersonal. Early in its history, all the "brothers" and "sisters" had been able to gather in one room for a staff meeting. Everyone could call everyone else by first name. But not now. There were no more meetings of the whole staff, and so many people had come in that it was nearly impossible to know names. To the extent that any sense of family remained, it was in smaller units rather than throughout the whole organization. At one time, the staff would get together for an annual "family reunion," a picnic designed to do nothing more than build and maintain relationships. It was all for fun. At other times, members of the family gathered to celebrate accomplishments and recognize triumphs,

186 LEADERSHIP AND SPIRIT

large and small. The celebrations helped build a sense of family. But the family reunions went the way of dinosaurs, and even the celebrations that involved the whole family slowly faded away. To the extent that celebrations continued, they also continued in individual work units. They were still important, but different.

The metaphor of family no longer works for the women and men of Composite, just as it no longer works in many organizations today. There are exceptions, of course. In TDIndustries, the company described in some detail in Chapter Two, the family metaphor still works. The company likes the metaphor and is intentional about fostering a sense of family. But in most companies, we need a new metaphor, another way to figuratively describe how we are, or can be, in relationship to each other.

I like the metaphor of community. Community reminds us of other words: of finding *commonalities* amid diversity, of deep and honest *communication*, of experiencing *connectedness*. Community works as a metaphor so long as we acknowledge and celebrate the gifts, skills, and perspectives we bring rather than long for sameness. In our work communities, we must find commonness and shared goals in the context of our differences, not in spite of them or in denial of them.

In contrast, words like *organization* and *corporation* stir up images of boxes on a chart with hard, straight lines connecting them; they speak of policies and procedures; they delineate lines of authority and responsibility. The word *organization* symbolizes hierarchy more than partnership, power over more than shared power, separation and distinction more than commonality. Executives are more important than supervisors, line is more important than staff, and so on.

The difference between these images and how we describe ourselves is important. The metaphors we have for the place where we work shape our thoughts and behavior, sometimes in ways we don't like, ways that we choose unwittingly. Our being and our behavior are likely to change if we understand ourselves as part of a community rather than as part of a corporation. Even how we understand and participate in the activity of leadership, and experience the presence of spirit, differs based on the metaphor we use. Organization defines place, communicates role, and delineates accountability and authority. Community invites—even elicits—broader and fuller participation. It holds before us the idea that leadership is shared and happens in a collective.

It is time to acknowledge the importance of community, to claim it as our new metaphor. It is time to turn our workplace into the community for which we yearn.

The Learning Organization and Community

Being a community and being a learning organization are linked. I won't attempt to identify all aspects of a learning organization as defined by Peter Senge and others, but I believe another reason community is important is that learning organizations and community are linked. They go hand in glove.

Learning organization has become a well-known phrase in our culture, but its meaning remains somewhat obscure. "Along with total quality management and process reengineering, 'organizational learning' has become a buzzword," says Senge. "But there is no such thing as a learning organization . . . when I speak of learning organization, I'm articulating a view that involves us—the observers—as much as the observed in a common system" (1995, p. 49). Developing a learning organization is grounded in the notion of community; as we develop one, we develop the other.

There are several reasons why this is true. In a learning organization, individuals focus on the broad and systemic implications of their actions, not simply on how a particular decision or action affects them. The impact on community is understood to be as important as the impact on self. Interdependencies are acknowledged and considered. As we learn to think and act systemically, we develop a learning organization while fostering community. Too, the process of dialogue that is a critical part of being a learning organization (a process described in Chapter Seven) builds a learning organization while it builds community. In Senge's words, "dialogue weaves a common fabric and connects them (individuals) at a deep level of being" (1995, p. 50). Becoming a learning organization also requires that we accept our differences rather than push for sameness, that we hold conflicts rather than try to hide them or too quickly resolve them, that we share our assumptions rather than simply act on them. Each of these builds community.

There is also a link between a learning organization and the understanding and practice of leadership that we call partnership. Senge describes it best:

> One reason that the myth of the great leader is so appealing is that it absolves us of the responsibility for developing leadership capabilities more broadly. In a learning organization, the burden is shifted: a perceived need for leadership (symptom) can be met by developing leadership capacities throughout the organization (fundamental solution), not by just relying on a hero leader (symptomatic solution). Success in finding a hero leader reinforces a belief in the group's powerlessness, thus making the fundamental solution more difficult. . . . Leading takes on new meanings in learning organizations. The leaders are those building the new organization and its capabilities . . . such leadership is inevitably collective [1995, p. 50].

Learning organizations and partnerships are both rooted in an understanding that leadership happens in relationships or in a community; developing one supports developing the other.

Community and Spiritual Development

Community development and spiritual development are interwoven. Spiritual development has two important dimensions: we must take the journey down and in and embrace the monsters—our fears and our insecurities—on the journey toward our hidden wholeness. And we must recognize and honor the hunger that self has for connectedness and community. Our whole self can be known only through an inner journey *and* through an outer experience of community. Given this, any experience that fosters inner awareness and outer connectedness is leadership development; understood in this way, leadership development is spiritual development. They are cut from the same cloth.

Leadership development as spiritual development happens in communities that are learning organizations. When a group of individuals come together and risk vulnerability, surface assumptions, engage in the kind of deep dialogue that allows meaning to flow from and through them, experience wholeness that honors and incorporates diversity, and hold conflict, they and the organization *learn*, they develop *community*, they engage in *partnership*, and they develop *spiritually*. As pointed out earlier, spiritual development sometimes happens in solitude as we take our journey down and in through prayer, meditation, journaling, or other individual activities. But some of our spiritual development takes place in the context of community and in the process of engagement with others.

Fostering Community

But how do we foster community? What can we do to cultivate it? How do we help our workgroups and organizations move toward the community we want and need? Does it really need to be fostered? Doesn't community sometimes just happen?

There are times when community does seem to happen on its own; we recognize it (often in retrospect) more than we intentionally build it. There are some who believe that this is the only way community can happen: naturally and effortlessly. This belief is predicated on an assumption that community comes to us as a gift.

Although I have occasionally experienced community as a gift, there are other times when I have found that community must be intentionally and purposefully fostered if it is to happen. Though it cannot be decreed or imposed, there are things that can be done to nurture and nourish it. In no certain order, I want to describe ways community naturally evolves, and other things we can do to nurture it.

Doing Real Work

The first way in which community is built is as real work is done. It evolves as crises and challenges are faced. A workgroup that has to respond to the challenge of starting a new organization, or turning around an old one, or that has to deal with the unexpected death of a colleague, or that goes through the trauma of a downsizing together, or that has to meet the challenge of getting a new product to market in record time, often finds that a sense of interconnectedness and spirit has been fostered in the process. A group that perceives that it is under siege, from external competitors or internal pressures, often experiences a sense of connectedness and community as they respond together to the threat. The great groups identified by Bennis and Biederman (recall Chapter Four) faced these kinds of challenges and crises.

Community is sometimes forged on the anvil of hardship. Individuals develop a sense of connectedness in response to the hardship, and both they and the community discover new vitality and energy, a new sense of spirit, in the process.

But crises and challenges are not the only real-work situations in which community is forged. Individuals who share power and work interdependently toward accomplishing a shared goal can, over time, be transformed from a workgroup into a community. A vision that is great enough, a mission that is compelling enough, and a set of shared values that is inclusive enough call individuals into connectedness and community.

This is what happened in the early days of Composite. Individual employees felt a deep resonance between their values and those of the company. The mission of Composite was the mission of its women and men; there was no disconnect between an individual's sense of purpose and the organization's purpose. It was easy for employees to think of themselves as family.

This is what still happens today in organizations like the Human Service Alliance (HSA), the nonprofit organization described in Chapter Four. The vision and purpose of this service organization, and the norms HSA has developed around partnership-as-leadership, foster community and spirit. Individuals are important at HSA; individuals learn and grow from their involvement. Community is equally important; it is naturally fostered as real work is done.

It also happens in for-profit organizations—SAS, W. L. Gore, Southwest Airlines, and many others. The shared goals, the pervasive sense that people are in this together, the sense of accountability that exists across levels and functions all enhance the possibility that individuals will experience being part of something larger, of being part of community.

The important thing to realize is that community evolves during accomplishment of the real work of the organization. Community development, like the development of individual leadership skills and perspectives, does not have to happen away from work. It can and does happen in the midst of it.

Community building also happens in work activities other than routine. Several years ago, the staff of the Center for Creative Leadership, for which I work, raised money and built a Habitat for Humanity house. It was partnership-in-action. There was no executive-as-leader. The whole of the experience was an act of cocreation; leadership emerged from the reciprocity of the relationships; it evolved from the collective. Individuals had various gifts, and they used them. As far as I know, no one thought when we started this project that a reason for doing it was to build community, and we did nothing during the process to intentionally make it happen. But it was one of the important, unintended consequences of our work together. Community evolved effortlessly, from the process of our being and doing together. Women and men came from throughout the organization, from every level and functional area, and worked together Saturdays and some weekdays, putting up vinyl siding, crawling on the roof and nailing shingles, painting the walls and woodwork, and finally doing the landscaping. In the process, relationships were built and community developed.

Working together, accomplishing important tasks, in the workplace or in the community is one way that community building appears to be naturally occurring. We respond to a crisis or challenge, or we engage in important work that calls forth the best we have within us, and we discover (perhaps retrospectively) that our sense of community has been developed.

These communities may not last beyond completion of the task or accomplishment of a particular goal, but this does not lessen their importance. We need community, and we do experience it (at least on occasion) in the places we work. Those times when we experience it become important reference points for us as to how we can be and do together.

Play

A second way to nurture community is through play. I recently completed the first phase of a team-development process with the eight top executives of a large company. The organization had been formed some three months prior from the merger of two companies having very dissimilar products, strategies, cultures, and practices of leadership. From the phone interviews I conducted with each executive before beginning my work with the team, it was clear that some relationships among individuals were solid, some were just forming, and others were shaky at best. Trust had not been developed; questions, even suspicions about others, were evident.

The team-development process that was used was designed to carefully and intentionally foster community. And it did. But in hindsight, the most important community-building event seems to have been the play, the rather serious play in the conference center's game room, that the executives engaged in after one of our long days of work. By their own report, they laughed, told stories, played darts and table shuffleboard, and closed the game room at two; in today's parlance, they bonded. None of these executives said they did this to foster community. They were simply ready to relax and blow off steam. But as they told their stories the next morning, it was clear that a sense of community had developed.

As experienced by these executives, play does more than provide welcome relief from a focus on tasks and a preoccupation with doing. It helps us see these tasks in new ways. It helps us develop altered perspectives. It helps us get beyond formal and often stereotyped roles to meet the real person who is our colleague. If in our doing we hit an impasse or stalemate, or if our relationships need unfreezing, play can help us thaw out and break through to new and deeper levels of understanding.

Play also gives new life and vitality to work communities. Play is structured into organizational activities such as annual picnics, end-of-the-week TGIF parties, and company softball teams. At other times, it is more spontaneous; it bursts forth, perhaps with a single word of irreverence that catalyzes playful kidding, or sharing a Dilbert cartoon, or good-natured teasing. These forms of play lead to connectedness and community so long as others are not trivialized in the process, so long as we are not using others as an "it," as the butt of our jokes.

"Aesthetic Competency"

We also cultivate community through "aesthetic competencies." The notion that there might be a connection between leadership development and art, and between community development and art, recently took on new meaning for me. Several years ago, I read Max De Pree's *Leadership Is an Art* and *Leadership Jazz* and heard Peter Vaill talk about "leadership as a performing art." But still I did not make the connection at anything more than a cognitive level. I even knew that colleagues at the Center for Creative Leadership had developed and were leading a new program called

"Leading Creatively," which was designed to use certain aesthetic competencies—such as drawing, collage, music making, and collaborative inquiry—to foster development of individual leadership capacities. But still the connection between art and fostering community remained nothing more than another idea running around in my head.

Then, for the third consecutive year, I participated in a conference designed to engage people in reflection and dialogue about the link between leadership and spirit. This third conference was different, at least for me. As I reflected on the conference, I realized that this one had more movement, music, poetry, and storytelling—more use of aesthetics—than the previous two. More than at any other time, I experienced the power of the arts to foster a sense of connectedness and community. Part of the power of aesthetic competencies is that they engage our whole self and use all of our energies (mental, physical, emotional, and spiritual) while at the same time building a sense of connectedness.

Art does not take the place of logic and rational analysis; it complements it. As two colleagues, Charles Palus and David Horth, say: "Constructing something [for our purposes, a sense of community] that has never been built before requires the two great engines of human creativity: analysis and artistry. The first works by formulas; it depends on generating and coordinating parts. The second works by perception and composition; it strives intuitively for original wholes" (1998, p. 7).

Perhaps you have already learned the power of aesthetic competency from your experience, in one setting or another; or perhaps you are not ready yet to experience it and don't think the place you work is ready to use movement or music or other art forms to foster community. Indeed, many organizations aren't ready. But if you are interested though not sure your organization is, think of small ways that you can introduce aesthetics into your small corner of the organization. And remember there are other ways to foster community, including additional means mentioned in this chapter.

Pay Attention

As a fourth means of fostering community, we can pay attention to our being and our doing. There are ways each of us can be, and things each of us can do, in real-work situations to foster community. Even when a mission is shared, values are in sync, and goals are agreed upon, community does not always automatically happen. Shared mission, values, and goals are important, but they are not always sufficient. At times, community formation requires attention to our being and our doing. Individual development and community development are linked.

Earlier we talked about how knowing ourselves is important to the understanding and practice of partnerships. Ways of knowing and being ourselves were described in detail in Chapters Five and Six, so here I highlight two aspects of our being that are particularly important to cultivating community.

First, so long as we remain unaware of what goes on deep inside, so long as we refuse to acknowledge our demons—our fears and insecurities—we continue to project them onto individuals and workgroups. On the one hand, the shadows we project keep communities from seeing the light of day. On the other hand, by developing inner awareness and learning to embrace the shadow, we are better able to foster community.

Second, when we use our gifts, claim our personal power, move from collusion to courage, and learn to "tell the truth without blame or judgment" (as Arrien says), we help a group move from what M. Scott Peck has called "pseudocommunity" to community. As the word suggests, pseudocommunity has a lot of pretense to it. In a pseudocommunity, individuals are polite and correct in a strained sort of way. They compromise important values or deeply held beliefs for the sake of getting along, they allow their identity to be lost in the group, and they say yes when they want to say no. In real community, we are ourselves—our real selves—and others are also. We foster community by using all of our energies not simply because it is the right thing to do, but because in doing so we become whole and free men and women and connect more fully to others.

We also foster community by paying attention to our doing, by using new skills and behaviors. The skills that help us build partnerships also help augment community. These ways of doing were described in detail in Chapter Seven, so again I simply highlight them here:

- Honoring diversity helps build community. We honor diversity because we know we need to enlarge our limited view of things, and in the process we enhance community.

- Holding conflict fosters community. We welcome and hold conflict rather than ignore or suppress it because we know that others have views as valid as our own, and needs as important as our own, and we trust that in holding conflict we can find better answers for all of us.

- Engaging in dialogue encourages community. *Dia-logos*, you'll remember, implies a "free-flowing of information through a group, allowing the group to attain insights that are not available individually" (Senge, 1990, pp. 10, 247). It is through the use of dialogue, whereby new truths are discovered and new meaning is made of tough and ambiguous situations, that partnerships and community emerge.

- Speaking for self and deep listening enhance community. Speaking for self is a way to claim our power, maintain our authenticity, and speak our truths without being judgmental or without blaming others. Deep listening is a way of honoring others, encouraging them to speak their truths, and creating understanding. Using both skills builds partnerships and community.

Structure and Systems

Another aspect of evolving community is that *organizations encourage or discourage it through structures and systems*. In a lunchtime conversation with a colleague several months ago, he described himself as a "structural determinist." He believes that structure determines behavior, including leadership behavior. He also believes that any organizational problem can be solved through structural solutions. His intervention in any work community would start with a structural perspective, with a focus on whether the community was effectively and efficiently organized to accomplish its work. I am not a structural determinist. I don't think structure determines behavior, but I do think it has an impact, often more than we know.

In the early part of the 1990s, Bolman and Deal "sorted insights from both research and practice into four major ways that both academics and practitioners make sense of organizations" (1991, p. 15). One of the four frames or lenses that they identified is the structural, and it is through this lens that I believe many executives and managers view their organization. But they look through it without observing the impact of structure on the understanding and practice of leadership, and without consciously noticing that the lens filters in as well as filters out. What's filtered out and what's filtered in are both important to community.

The structural frame filters in the importance of formal roles and relationships. When operating through this frame, structures are developed, roles are defined and clarified, responsibilities are allocated, and policies and procedures are developed. Each of these is important; used wisely, they lead to efficient and productive work in an organization and create possibilities for community to happen. If overused or misused, they stifle spirit and discourage community.

What's filtered out, especially if the structural frame is overused, is any focus on people, the importance of the symbolic or the spiritual, or the impact of structure on practices of leadership. Let me give one example. A friend works in an organization that recently completed a substantial restructuring, one that affected most people in the company. One of the company's senior executives told this friend that they did the restructuring without regard to its impact on people or the culture of the organization. Those involved in the planning of the new organization (they were but a few, and all were senior executives) were determined to make sure that the boxes got put in the right places. Efficiency was more important than effectiveness, control more important than commitment, clear definition of roles and responsibilities more important than culture and community. Though not intended, the structure that evolved discouraged the use of partnerships and eliminated the possibility of community.

Picture a typical organization chart with straight lines and boxes, one in which functional areas are separated and individual roles are clearly demarcated. Imagine the impact on partnerships and community. Compare this picture with the organizational chart at Southwest Airlines, where, according to Kelleher, the chart is turned upside down. Or picture the organization chart at TDIndustries, turned on its side. Go one step further and look through yet another lens: picture an organization chart that looks weblike rather than full of straight lines and boxes, an organization chart that depicts interdependencies and not simply individual responsibilities. Imagine the impact that each structure might have on the practice of leadership and development of community. For me, the first picture, the typical one, is rather dispiriting and does not call images of community to mind. The others do, some more than others.

Partnership-as-leadership and the related need for community have implications for how we structure organizations. Structure does not have to be associated with "red tape, mindless memos, and rigid bureaucrats" (Bolman and Deal, 1991, p. 77). Structure does not have to separate people, create some who are more than and some who are less than, or divide functions. Structure does not have to suffocate spirit or discourage community. Instead, structure can encourage collaboration and community. If leadership is understood and practiced as partnerships, and if individuals and community are to be interwoven, organizational structures must be supportive. Supportive structures look like a web of interlocking functions and people. Collaboration is structured in and unnecessary and harmful competition are structured out; competition is the antithesis of community. There is more coordination from the side than from the top. With coordination from the side (or, if you will, from the center of the web), managers and executives act as partners rather than bosses.

Policies and standard operating procedures, like structures, either encourage or discourage community. Earlier, I mentioned a manager I worked with who wanted to create policies and procedures to cover every possible work situation, no matter how minute or unimportant. The sheer volume of policies she created was suffocating. For her, managing policies was easier than managing people. In my experience, she is not alone in her wish to manage by policy manual. Managing people gets messy; in contrast, managing policies seems clean and easy.

The problem is that as we create more policies, more practices, more rules, a larger and thicker SOP manual. We also create what Gordon MacKenzie recently termed a "giant hairball." He worked at Hallmark Cards for some thirty years, eventually shaping a position in which he was responsible for creative paradox (a title, I confess, that I do not fully understand). Along the way, he noticed that every new policy or procedure added a new hair to a corporate hairball. "Hairs are never taken away," he says, "only added. Even frequent reorganizations have failed to remove hairs (people, sometimes; hairs, never). Quite the contrary, each reorganization seems to add a whole *new layer of hairs*. The hairball grows enormous" (1996, p. 31).

Before long, and without anyone really noticing it or intending for it to happen, the hairball becomes large enough and powerful enough that it represents a "Gordian Knot of Corporate Normalcy (i.e., conformity with the *accepted model, pattern or standard* of the corporate mind set)" (1996, p. 30). The problem is, the bigger the hairball the more spirit tends to be snuffed out. It is hard, if not impossible, to create community, honor spirit, and practice partnership-as-leadership if the hairball gets too large.

Other organizational systems, such as performance-appraisal and compensation systems, also encourage or discourage partnerships and communities. Too often, organizations say they want strong team effort, collaboration across functional areas, and people pulling together to accomplish organizational goals, but they still reward individual performance. By and large, performance-appraisal systems are designed to appraise the past performance of individuals, and to establish individual performance goals for the future, rather than to assess the effectiveness of one form of partnership or another. If partnerships are to work, and if community is to be fostered, these important human resource systems must be supportive and encouraging.

How can an organization know if its systems and structures and policies are fostering community? Here are some questions to ask:

- How inclusively is information shared? Conversely, are there organizational secrets known only by a few?
- Do structures and systems encourage sharing of power and control?
- Do structures and systems foster interdependence and community activity as much as they encourage individual initiative?
- Do structures and systems encourage organizational learning?
- Is the organization moving toward or away from understanding leadership as an activity in which all are involved?
- Do structures and systems leave room for spirit to shape individuals and foster interconnectedness and community?

Celebrate

My next-to-last suggestion of a way in which we foster community is through celebrations and rituals. Executives and managers tend to operate on the assumption that the recipe for success is one part strategy, structure, and systems mixed with an equal part individual leadership skills. This glue, they think, bonds people and ensures business success. Everything else, including celebrations, is ancillary to these more rational and logical processes. Celebrations might be a nice thing to do if there is time after the real work of the company is done, but they are not necessary, not a critical ingredient in the recipe for success. So the thinking seems to go.

Just as baking powder is a leavening agent in many food recipes, so celebration is an important leavening agent in organizations. Celebrations lighten the work experience and give us a sense of buoyancy. They summon spirit. They foster connectedness and help us build community. They help us remember purpose, stay connected to core values, and honor work that has been done together.

In his latest book (this one written with M. K. Key), Terry Deal says, "The ups and downs, comings and goings, triumphs and mishaps of corporate life *must be* punctuated periodically with ceremonial event. Otherwise, the collective spirit that unites people begins to wither and wane" (1998, p. 5). I put the *must be* in italics to stress that celebration is not an option; it is a key ingredient in the recipe for success. "People have feelings, heart, soul, spirit and other nonrational qualities," write Deal and Key. "When organizations speak to these, people voluntarily give their all. When the workplace ignores these nonrational qualities, people typically check out. They leave, go on strike, sabotage or—more passively— go through the motions" (1998, p. x).

Celebrations are important to community building and organizational success, but not if they are carried out as perfunctory, let's-go-through-the-motions-and-get-this-thing-over events. Celebrations are not a leavening agent, and they don't summon spirit if they are devoid of meaning or purpose. We have all experienced celebrations like this. One large corporation I know, has over the past several years been through several significant downsizings (an executive of this company said "we tried to cut the tail off the cat one inch at a time"). Accompanying the downsizing, they adopted provisions of the new employment contract (which we discussed in Chapter Three). Not long after one of the downsizings, the company held a long-planned banquet to celebrate those employees who had twenty-five years of tenure with the company. At an earlier time, when the company could proudly proclaim its life-time employment practices, this celebration was meaningful. But now it was experienced as empty and purposeless.

To encourage partnerships and foster community, organizations must pay attention to what's celebrated. They must celebrate accomplishment of team efforts, honor results that come from interdependent and collaborative action, and acknowledge attainment of shared goals. In the past, we have honored individuals and anointed them as heroes or heroines, without remembering significant contributions of the entire work community. In the process, we undercut the sense of community we want to foster. Bonds are developed and community is built as contributions of the entire community are celebrated.

Rituals are also an important way to foster community. Life in community is triumph and failure, gain and loss, winning and losing. It is starting new programs and practices while we let go of others, organizing into new ways of working together while saying goodbye to old ones. It is an important part of community life to have rituals that help us let go of practices, programs, and structures that no longer serve us well, as well as rituals that help us embrace new ones.

Rituals can also help say goodbye and hello to colleagues; used wisely, they cultivate community. As with programs and processes, women and men are constantly moving in and out of work communities. A manager gets promoted, a next-door office neighbor leaves for a promising future with another company, a coworker decides to stay home with young children, a colleague dies, new employees are hired, managers transition into new positions within the work community. Using rituals can ease, and help us make meaning of, these transitions.

Not too long ago, a colleague who left our organization wanted to slip out quietly, to exit without any ritual or ceremony. Because this was a strongly stated preference, he was allowed to depart without any formal goodbyes. What might have been best for him was not best for the community. Members of the work community could not get closure on a relationship that was important; they were left with unfinished business. Emotionally and spiritually, it is important to say goodbye.

In contrast, several years ago a deeply admired and respected member of our organization died after a courageous battle with cancer. Not long after his death, everyone in the organization who wished to do so gathered at work one afternoon to celebrate his life by telling stories and sharing memories. It was a warm, moving, healing experience. It was a spiritual experience. For me, the presence of spirit weaving through and among those who participated was palatable. It was an experience that fostered community.

We also need rituals that help us say hello. The first several months after a new person joins an organization are pivotal. Norms are set, relationships are developed, membership—or lack of it—in the workgroup is established. Even those organizations having a prescribed checklist that a supervisor or manager uses to acquaint a new hire with the details of the job often have no formal rituals by which to welcome the newcomer into the community. Managers who transition into responsibility for a new workgroup seldom engage in any significant ritual to ease the process and nurture connectedness and community.

Celebrations and rituals are examples of what we do when we view an organization from another of the frames identified by Bolman and Deal, the symbolic frame. According to those authors (1991), the symbolic frame—also called the "expressive" or "spiritual" frame—is the newest and least developed of the four frames; from my experience, it is the one that managers and executives tend to use the least. For our purposes (fostering the kind of community in which room is left for spirit and true partnership can happen), it may well be the most important.

One of the reasons that the symbolic frame is less understood and appreciated is that it does not have the rational basis that appears in the other frames (such as the structural, described earlier). Viewed through the symbolic lens, "organizations are cultures that are propelled more by rituals, ceremonies, heroes, and myths than by rules, policies, and managerial authority" (Bolman and Deal, 1991, pp. 15–16).

Those in management positions who are structural determinists, who believe that policies can be created and used to cover every situation, who think goals and objectives once set should remain immutable, and who think that they can create order out of the turbulence of permanent white water, are not as likely to view their organization through the symbolic lens.

But those who know from experience that white water is real and constant, that work at times has to get done amid chaos, who understand that cause and effect are not always linked, who have learned that policies and procedures and rationality are not always sufficient to respond to all the uncertainties and ambiguities of organizational life, and who know that they must be nimble enough to change goals in response to changing conditions are more likely to look to symbolic events such as ceremonies and rituals to provide a source of meaning.

Most managers and executives, I hasten to add, fit neither of these caricatures. Most blend the extremes; they know that both the analytical and the symbolic are important. I describe them as I do to make the point that some see little reason for focusing on the symbolic while others know of its importance.

Ceremonies and rituals are not the only way to use the symbolic and nurture the spiritual side of organizations. Using play (mentioned earlier) and telling stories (mentioned next) are other ways of using the symbolic frame and fostering community.

Tell Stories

Finally, we foster community through using stories. Our lives are stories. Each individual life is a story, and life in a work community is a story. Stories are powerful. Remembering them and telling them helps us stay in touch with important truths about ourselves and important truths about our community.

In workgroups and organizations, stories help us move toward partnership-as-leadership and foster community. As we tell stories of team-leadership working, stories that recognize the value of bosses and subordinates who act as partners, stories that describe groups effectively and successfully learning to cocreate a shared goal and work toward it interdependently, we nurture community. (Conversely, if we only tell stories of heroic individual achievement, we reinforce the executive-as-leader model of leadership.)

Stories are a powerful medium for creating and making meaning of our lives in work communities. Because leadership means, in part, making sense of the variety of often complex and ambiguous experiences, stories can help us in our meaning-making process. How to make sense of the budgeting process? By telling stories of how money has been spent that conveys the meaning that it has for the community. How to make sure that we make sense of our mission and purpose? By telling stories of how individuals and groups fulfill the communities mission and purpose. Want to reinforce the importance of exquisite customer service? Tell stories.

Stories communicate deeply held individual and organizational values. Listen to the stories that are told in an organization, about who and what gets reinforced and rewarded and who and what gets ignored, and you can identify an organization's core values. At times, the values that surface in stories are not consistent with those mounted in plexiglass and hung around the office, but the values we learn from the stories that are told shape our behavior, for better or worse. Stories are maps that guide our thoughts and behavior.

Stories reinforce culture. One important task carried out by sages—wise men and women who have been around for a while—is telling stories about the organization's history. From them we can learn how the company's norms (the way we do things around here) evolved; we can learn from the mistakes of the past, and we can better understand the present and where we want to go in the future. So much of a company's history and culture are carried in the heads and hearts of its people that without their stories we have no way of learning and keeping alive important traditions and norms.

In the American Red Cross, an organization I have been privileged to work in for the past several years, stories are told to reinforce important traditions and values. Stories are told about people from the past, like Clara Barton, founder of the American branch of the Red Cross, whose courage and uncommon devotion and service made her a person worth remembering and emulating. Stories are told about present volunteers who give unselfishly of their time and energy to assist those experiencing a disaster. The people of the American Red Cross appreciate the power of stories.

Telling our individual stories is as important to fostering community as is telling the organization's story. As we take time to share our past, relate our own learning from experience, describe the values that have been forged on our own anvil of hardship, and tell our story of life in the organization, we foster connectedness and community. As we openly acknowledge the monsters we have encountered and attempted to embrace on our inner journey, as we tell our story of meeting the stranger who is the self, as we share the experience of discerning and claiming our gifts—or even the attempt to do so, successful or not—we build relationships and nurture community. As we tell stories of work that gives us energy, work we've done that is reflective of deeply held personal values, work that calls forth the best we have within us, we encourage others to do the same and we nourish community. These personal stories are deeply meaningful and deeply powerful.

Stories—those that are personal and those that are organizational—tell us where we have been and point us to where we might want to go. In a recent presentation and conversation, Ray Heiden, a professor at the University of Illinois and a master storyteller, reminded those of us in attendance of an obvious truth that has not-so-obvious implications: all stories have a beginning, a middle, and an end. We are always in the middle of our story, and we join an organization in the middle of its story. Our story and the stories we hear about our organization's past help us understand what we are experiencing today, and they help us better understand where we want to go tomorrow. The middle of any story makes sense if we understand what went before and what comes after.

Finally, stories promote the weaving together of leadership, spirit, and community. If we experience this weaving together, both individuals and organizations will find a new energy and vitality, which creates a ripple effect into other communities in which we live and to which we belong.

If, by chance, we don't like where we are in the middle of the individual or organizational story, we can change it. The Epilogue details the choices we must make to change our story, to change it so we might experience spirit breathing new energy and vitality into us and our organizations.

Epilogue
Rewriting the End of Our Story

I shall be telling this with a sigh
Somewhere ages and ages hence:
Two roads diverged in a wood, and I—
I took the one less traveled by,
And that has made all the difference.

—Robert Frost (in Sullivan, 1988, p. 142)

In a strict sense, this is an epilogue; in a broader sense, it isn't. Like other epilogues, the purpose of this last, brief chapter is to round out or complete this book.

But in another sense, this book and the story told in it are not yet complete. To repeat what I said in the Preface, I realize as I finish this book that I am in the middle of the story. Over the years, I have learned a lot about understandings and practices of leadership and the impact of those various practices on spirit. But there's still a lot I don't know. One of the things I don't know is how the story of the weaving together of leadership and spirit will end. From my perspective, that story is just beginning.

But I do know there are countless men and women in this country today who are asking questions about the link between leadership and spirit, between work and spirit. They, like you and me, want work to provide a sense of meaning and purpose, want to use all of their energies in their work and in their leadership activities, want to overcome the disconnect between how they see themselves as people and how they see themselves as workers. They want leadership processes to be inspiriting, not dispiriting. They are in the middle of their story.

That is also where I assume you are in your story. Even though you have almost finished this book, I assume you are not yet finished with your story, that you can and will change the story of your personal journey, and I hope that you will join with the countless others who are adding their threads to the tapestry of leadership and spirit. As you do this, you help cocreate a better ending for all of us.

What's important now, as we consider the story, is to know the choices we must make, to know which roads we must take, if leadership and spirit are to be interwoven. Here are some of those choices:

- We must choose courage over collusion. The latter road is easier, but the former is the road we must take.

- We must choose interdependence over dependence or counterdependence. We must know and be ourselves and be part of community. We must be both-and people.

- We must choose collaboration over competition. Collaboration is a road less traveled, but it is time to travel it.

- We must choose community over hierarchy. We must move toward community in our own small corner of the organization, even if the larger organization remains unchanged.

- We must take the inner journey to embrace the shadow. This is the road least traveled of all. But we can no longer afford to pretend that our shadow doesn't exist, or that it is benign. Remember, this road leads through the wilderness; there is no way around it. We must travel this path all the way in and down.

- We must choose to understand and be our true self and our whole self. We must never settle for being a caricature.

- We must discern, claim, and use our gifts in the activity of leadership.

- We must forgo the road that leads to coercive power—even though it is a fine seduction—and take the path toward personal power. In the end, it is the path worth traveling, the one that leads to personal renewal and partnership-as-leadership.

- We must quit looking for heroic leaders. We have taken that road in the past. But it is a new day, and new roads lie open before us. It is time to take the road toward partnerships. On this road, we learn to be accountable and responsible even if we do not have authority.

- We must choose to use all of our energies—mental, physical, emotional, and spiritual—in our work and in the activity of leadership. We must learn to see with the "eye of contemplation," to discern the movement of spirit within and among us. This is a different road than what many of us have traveled, or at least a different way of traveling on the road, but it is here that we find a wellspring of energy and vitality.

Making these choices is not easy. The old roads that we have more frequently traveled are familiar and thus appear easier to traverse. When we choose the road less traveled, we know that because it is a new road our pace is slower, at least initially. Because we have tried other new roads before, we know that we find detours and dead ends. We even know that at times we go in reverse. On one part of the journey—the journey in and down—we know that we have to befriend our monsters, and it is not a pleasant thought. We can even guess that on this road less traveled there will be times when we don't feel up to the journey, that we don't think we have the skills or capacities needed to complete it.

So, again we ask: Why take it?

Because it is the road to self. Because it is the road to partnerships. Because on this road we experience spirit breathing new life into us and into leadership activities. Because it is the way for work to be worth the investment of our lives.

References

Arrien, A. *The Four-Fold Way*. San Francisco: Harper San Francisco, 1993.

Autry, J. *Love and Profit: The Art of Caring Leadership*. New York: Morrow, 1991.

Bellah, R. *Habits of the Heart*. New York: HarperCollins, 1985.

Bender, S. *Plain and Simple*. San Francisco: HarperCollins, 1989.

Bennis, W. *On Becoming a Leader*. Reading, Mass.: Addison-Wesley, 1989.

Bennis, W. "Cultivating Creative Genius." *Industry Week*, Aug. 18, 1997, p. 84.

Bennis, W., and Biederman, P. W. *Organizing Genius: The Secrets of Creative Collaboration*. Reading, Mass.: Addison-Wesley, 1997.

Block, P. *Stewardship*. San Francisco: Berrett-Koehler, 1993.

Bolman, L., and Deal, T. *Reframing Organizations*. San Francisco: Jossey-Bass, 1991.

Briskin, A. *The Stirring of Soul in the Workplace*. San Francisco: Jossey-Bass, 1996.

Brown, J., and Issacs, D. "Building Corporations as Communities." In K. Gozdz (ed.), *Community Building, Renewing Spirit, and Learning in Business*. San Francisco: New Leaders Press, 1995.

Buber, M. *I and Thou*. New York: Scribner, 1970.

Bunker, K., and Webb, A. *Learning How to Learn from Experience*. Greensboro, N.C.: Center for Creative Leadership, 1992.

Cheshire, A. *A Partnership of the Spirit*. Dallas, Tex.: TDIndustries, 1987.

Chopra, D. *The Seven Spiritual Laws of Success*. San Rafael, Calif.: Amber-Allen, 1994.

Collins, J. C., and Porras, J. *Built to Last*. New York: HarperBusiness, 1994.

Cory, D. "The Killing Fields: Institutions and the Death of Our Spirits." In L. Spears (ed.), *Insights on Leadership*. New York: Wiley, 1998.

Deal, T., and Key, M. K. *Corporate Celebration*. San Francisco: Berrett-Koehler, 1998.

De Pree, M. *Leadership Is an Art*. New York: Doubleday, 1989.

Drath, W. "Approaching the Future of Leadership Development." In C. McCauley, R. S. Moxley, and E. Van Velsor (eds.), *The Center for Creative Leadership Handbook of Leadership Development*. San Francisco: Jossey-Bass, 1998.

Drucker, P. *The Practice of Management*. New York: HarperCollins, 1954.

Freiberg, K., and Freiberg, J. *Nuts!* Austin, Tex.: Bard Press, 1996.

Galagan, P. "Measuring a Hidden Asset." *Training and Development Journal*, Sept. 1988, p. 37.

Handy, C. *The Age of Paradox*. Boston: Harvard Business School Press, 1994.

Handy, C. *The Hungry Spirit*. New York: Broadway Books, 1998.

Harvey, J. *The Abilene Paradox and Other Meditations on Management*. Lexington, Mass.: Heath, 1998.

Hesse, H. *Demian: The Story of Emil Sinclair's Youth*. (M. Roloff and M. Lebeck, trans.). New York: Bantam Books, 1965.

Hyde, M., and McGuiness, M. *Introducing Jung*. New York: Totem Books, 1994.

Jackson, P. *Sacred Hoops*. New York: Hyperion, 1995.

Jacobi, J. *The Psychology of C. J. Jung*. New Haven, Conn.: Yale University Press, 1973. (Originally published 1942.)

Jaworski, J. *Synchronicity: The Inner Path of Leadership*. San Francisco: Berrett-Koehler, 1996.

Johnston, W. *Workforce 2000: Work and Workers for the 21st Century*. Indianapolis: Hudson Institute, 1987.

Jung, C. G. *The Basic Writings of C. G. Jung*. (S. de Laszlo, ed.). New York: Modern Library, 1993. (Originally published 1959.)

Kabat-Zinn, J. *Wherever You Go There You Are*. New York: Hyperion, 1994.

Kaplan, B. *Beyond Ambition*. San Francisco: Jossey-Bass, 1991.

Kegan, R. *The Evolving Self*. Cambridge, Mass.: Harvard University Press, 1982.

Kelleher, H. "A Culture of Commitment." *Leader to Leader*, Spring 1997, pp. 20–24.

Lee, W. "A Conversation with Herb Kelleher." In F. Luthans (ed.), *Organizational Dynamics*. New York: American Management Association, 1994.

Leonard, G. *The Silent Pulse*. New York: Dutton, 1978.

Levering, R., and Moskowitz, M. "The 100 Best Companies to Work for in America." *Fortune*, Jan. 12, 1998, p. 84.

MacKenzie, G. *Orbiting the Great Hairball*. New York: Penguin Books, 1996.

Maslow, A. *Religion, Values, and Peak Experience*. New York: Penguin Books, 1970.

Noer, D. *Healing the Wounds*. San Francisco: Jossey-Bass, 1993.

Palmer, P. *The Active Life: Wisdom for Work, Creativity, and Caring*. New York, HarperCollins, 1990.

Palmer, P. *The Courage to Teach*. San Francisco: Jossey-Bass, 1998a.

Palmer, P. "Leading from Within." In L. Spears (ed.), *Insights on Leadership*. New York: Wiley, 1998b.

Palus, C., and Horth, D. "Leading Creatively." *Ideas into Action*, 1998, *18*(2), 7.

Pinchot, G. "An Alternative to Hierarchy." *Leader to Leader*, 1998, no. 10, pp. 41–46.

Plamondon, W. "Energy and Leadership." In F. Hesselbein (ed.), *The Leader of the Future*. San Francisco: Jossey-Bass, 1996.

Purdum, T. S. "Strike Threat at American Air Draws Clinton Plea." *New York Times*, Feb. 13, 1997, p. C22.

Rader, D. "What Really Makes Life Fun." *Parade*, Sept. 20, 1998, pp. 4–5.

Richards, D. *Artful Work*. San Francisco: Berrett-Koehler, 1995.

Rogers, C. *On Becoming a Person*. Cambridge, Mass.: Riverside Press, 1961.

Schaefer, C., and Darling, J. *Spirit Matters: Using Contemplative Disciplines in Work and Organizational Life*. Chestnut Ridge, N.Y.: High Tor Alliance, 1996.

Senge, P. *The Fifth Discipline*. New York: Doubleday, 1990.

Senge, P. "Creating Quality Communities." In K. Gozdz (ed.), *Community Building, Renewing Spirit, and Learning in Business*. San Francisco: New Leaders Press, 1995.

Sullivan, C. (ed.). *America in Poetry: With Paintings, Drawings, Photography, and Other Works of Art*. New York: Abrams, 1988.

Terkel, S. *Working*. New York: Pantheon Books, 1974.

Vaill, P. *Spiritual Leading and Learning*. San Francisco: Jossey-Bass, 1998.

Verespej, M. "Flying His Own Course." *Industry Week*, Nov. 20, 1995, pp. 22–24.

Weisbord, M. *Productive Workplaces: Organizing and Managing for Dignity, Meaning, and Community*. San Francisco: Jossey-Bass, 1991.

Whyte, D. *The Heart Aroused*. New York: Doubleday, 1994.

Wilber, K. *The Marriage of Sense and Soul*. New York: Random House, 1998.

Wills, G. *Certain Trumpets*. New York: Simon & Schuster, 1994.

Index

concepts and, 47–50; maintenance of, reasons for, 63–66; model of, 46, 49, 50; partnership-as-leadership versus, 71–72, 73–74, 101; physical offices of, 61; problems of, 63–64; shadows of, 55–60, 63, 137–140. *See also* Command-and-control leadership; Dispiriting leadership
Exodus, 141–143
Expectations of others, trying to meet, 109–111, 122–123
Experience of spirit, 27–30; community, 35–37; in companies, 37–39; everyday, 27–28, 29–30; internal, 30–32; interpersonal, 32–35; synchronicity and, 28–30
Expressive frame, 203–204
External focus, 32, 41; costs of, 130–133, 133–134; ignorance of inner life and, 129; ignorance of shadow and, 56–57
External influences on identity, 113–114
Extroverts, 144, 146
Eye of contemplation, 22, 211

F

Facilitator, for engaging in dialogue, 164
False self, 126–127, 210
Family metaphor: community metaphor and, 185–187; at "Composite Corporation," 7, 185–186, 190; at Southwest Airlines, 87; at TDIndustries, 38–39, 186
Fear: of chaos, 135, 139–140, 150; coercive power and, 51–52, 54; collusion and, 66; of conflict, 164–165; dispiriting effects of, 51–52, 54; embracing, 96–97; of inner-life development, 134
Fear-based leadership, 58, 59–60, 130–131; competitive worldview and, 139
Feedback, 112–113, 142, 148
Fiedler, F., 49
Firing decisions, 79–81
Flattened organization, 69, 82, 118
Followers: executive ego inflation and, 61–62; leadership models incorporating, 48–49, 50; partnership-building practices for, 173–179
Forcefulness, 98–99
Fortune, 100 best companies to work for in America, 89

Four-Fold Way (Arrien), 97
Fox, M., 24
Frame: structural, 197–198; symbolic, 203–204
Freiberg, J., 85, 87–88
Freiberg, K., 85, 87–88
Frost, R., 209
Functional atheism, 139, 150
Future Search Conferences, 169

G

Galagan, P., 18
Gandhi, M., 92
Gardening, 149
Gardner, J., 156
Gender differences, 52
General Electric (GE), 93
General Motors, 161
Gifts: claiming personal, 118–121, 210; community as, 189; heeding personal calling and, 123; honoring diversity of, 156–158, 196; of the inner journey, 149–151; versus knowledge and skills, 119–120; payoffs to honoring, 158; respect for individuals and their, 76, 92–93, 156–158
Goal orientation, 40
Goals and objectives, preparation of, 36–37
Goodbye, rituals or saying, 201–202
Gordian Knot of Corporate Normalcy, 199
Gordon, T., 159
Gore-Tex, 89
Great-man theory of leadership, 47–48; examples of leaders under, 92; partnership alternative to, 92–94, 211
Great workgroups, 81–82
Greenleaf, R., 143
Groupthink, 175
Guided visualization, 146

H

Habitat for Humanity, 191–192
Hairballs, 199
Hallmark Cards, 199
Handy, C., 3, 17, 109–110
Hardships, 134, 141, 143, 149, 190
Harvey, J., 65
Health and Wellness Project, 90
Heiden, R., 206–207

partnership-leadership, 72–73, 91–92, 117–118, 121
Internal constraints on spirit, 40–41; of executives-as-leaders, 55–64
Internal experience of spirit, 30–32
Internal influences on identity, 114–116
Interpersonal experience of spirit, 32–35
Interrupting, 160
Introverts, 144
"-isms," 9
Issacs, D., 182

J

Jackson, P., 16, 173
Jacobi, J., 55
"Jane" story, 120–121
Jaworski, J., 28–29
Jaworski, M., 28–29
Job-placement decisions, 157
Jogging, 149
Jordan, M., 173
Journaling, 31, 146
Jung, C. G., 29, 55, 109, 136, 137, 140–141, 144, 146

K

Kabat-Zinn, J., 145
Kaplan, B., 61
Kegan, R., 111
Kelleher, H., 85, 86, 87, 89, 198
Key, M. K., 201
King, M. L., Jr., 92
Knowledge workers, 67

L

Layoff-survivor sickness, 14–15
Layoffs, threat of, 95
Leader Effectiveness Training (LET), 159
Leadership: coercive power and, 50–52; command-and-control, 4–7, 11–12, 46; cultural differences in, 184; and followership, 48–49; forces of change for, 67–70; inner journey and, 151; models and concepts of, 47–50; partnership model of, 71–102; personal development for, 105–128; rationale for new practices in, 67–70; shared power and, 74; spirited versus dispirited, 39; synchronicity in, 29; that

constrains spirit, 43–70. *See also* Dispiriting leadership; Leadership-spirit link; Partnership-as-leadership
Leadership development, 48, 56, 125; and art, 193–194; as spiritual development, 189
Leadership, dispiriting. *See* Dispiriting leadership
Leadership Is an Art (De Pree), 193
Leadership Jazz (De Pree), 193
Leadership process, 168–171
Leadership selection, great-man theory and, 48
Leadership simulation, 174–175
Leadership skills and behaviors, 48–49
Leadership-spirit link, 8–10; art and, 194; bottom line and, 18–20, 88, 89; choices for embracing, 210–211; in community, 185; in companies, 39; internal experience of, 30; in partnership-as-leadership, 74–75, 101–102; questions about, 21–22. *See also* Dispiriting leadership; Leadership; Spirit
Leadership styles, shadow-driven, 57–60
Leadership team, 169
Leadership traits, 47–48
Learners, blocked, 106
Learning organization, 187–188, 189
Lee, W., 85, 86
LeFauvre, S., 161–162
Leider, R., 108
Leonard, G., 23, 183
Levering, R., 89
Lincoln, A., 47
Listening, deep, 147, 159–160, 162, 196
Lockheed skunk works, 81
Lowe, J., Sr., 37
Lombardi, V., 47
London Business School, 109
Lone Ranger, 184
Looking Glass simulation, 174–175

M

MacKenzie, G., 199
Maintenance behaviors, 48
Manhattan project, 81
Manifestations of spirit, 30–39. *See also* Experience of spirit; Spirit
"Martha" vignette, 43–44; compliance in, 51; partnership model applied to, 77–78

99–100; skills for, 158–167; spirit in, 74–75, 101–102; at TDIndustries, 38, 186; in teams, 81–84; in three vignettes, 77–81; urgency in, 98–99
Patton, G., 47
Paying attention, 159–160, 195–200
Peck, M. S., 195
Peer communities, 89–90
Performance: under hierarchy, 85; inner journey and enhancement of, 151; unacceptable, dealing with, 79–81, 178
Performance-appraisal systems, 199–200
Perks, executive, 61, 62
Permanent white water: need for whole self in, 13; reemergence of community in, 181–183; symbolic frame and, 204
Perot, R., 16
Persona: defined, 55, 137; shadow and, 55–60, 137
Personal development, 105–128; being-doing balance and, 107–109; heed one's call and, 122–124; of inner life, 129–152; self-awareness for, 109–121; willingness to change and, 105–107. *See also* Identity; Individuation; Inner journey; Self; Self-awareness
Personal growth workshops, 148–149
Personal life stories, sharing of, 147
Personal power: claiming, 96–98, 154–155, 211; coercive power versus, 94–98, 154–155; as gift of inner journey, 151; in partnerships, 75, 94–98; personal gifts and, 121; speaking for self and, 161
Personality preferences, 143–144
Physical energy, 8, 13, 14, 125
Physical offices of executives, 61
Pinchot, G., 43, 182
Plain and Simple (Bender), 27
Plamondon, W., 70
Play, community building through, 192–193, 204
Playground partnerships, 73
Policies, supportive of partnership and community, 199
Porras, J., 93
Power: balance of, 75; coercive, 50–52, 94–96, 154; naïve view of, 94–98; personal, 94–98, 154–155; shared, in partnerships, 74, 75, 94–98; and staying quiet about conflict, 165. *See also* Coercive power

Prayer, 32, 145–146
Prejudices, 59
Present, being: executives', 159; followers', 176–178
Presidents of the United States, persona and shadow of, 55–56
Proactive versus reactive, 155
Problem focus, 160
Process, tending to the, 168–171
Projection, 59, 60, 130–133, 138–140, 142. *See also* Shadow
Pseudocommunity, 195–196
Punishments, in coercive power, 50, 96
Purdum, T. S., 54

Q

Quaker clearness committees, 147
Quality focus, 69–70
Questions, asking, 160

R

Racism, 9
Rader, D., 138
Rationalism, 22, 25–26, 194
Real-work situations: community building in, 190–192; partnership participation in, 76–77, 177–178
Reality of spirit, 25–26
Reciprocity of relationships, 72
Reflection, 31; disciplines of, 145–146; for inner journey, 143–146; personality preferences for, 143–144
Reframing Organizations (Bolman and Deal), 175
Relationship skills, 158–167
Relationships: one-to-one, 77–81; reciprocity of, 72; spirit experienced in, 32–35. *See also* Partnership-as-leadership
Religion, spirit and, 24–25, 26
Resentment, 54, 78
Resistance, command-and-control leadership and, 51
Respect for personhood, 76, 156–158
Respite Care Projects, 90
Responsibility: belief in ultimate individual, 139, 150; choosing, 211; coercive power and, 51–52; collusion and, 64–66; personal power and, 155; shared, in partnerships, 75–76, 86. *See also* Accountability

This Page Constitutes a
Continuation of the Copyright Page

More Titles from the Center for Creative Leadership

Positive Turbulence
Developing Climates for Creativity, Innovation, and Renewal
Stanley S. Gryskiewicz

Can your company manage–even encourage–turbulence in ways that actually strengthen its competitive stance? Absolutely. Top organizational psychologist Stanley Gryskiewicz argues that challenges to the status quo can be catalysts for creativity, innovation, and renewal and shows leaders how they can keep their company on the competitive edge. Developed through the author's work with many of the world's leading companies over the course of thirty years, *Positive Turbulence* delivers proven methods for creating an organization that continuously renews itself.

Hardcover   2224 pages   Item #E952 $32.95

Maximizing the Value of 360-Degree Feedback
A Process for Successful Individual and Organizational Development
Walter Tornow, Manuel London, & CCL Associates, Center for Creative Leadership

In this unprecedented volume, CCL draws upon twenty-eight years of leading research and professional experience to deliver the most thorough, practical and accessible guide to 360-degree feedback ever. Readers will discover precisely how they can use 360-degree feedback as a tool for achieving a variety of objectives such as communicating performance expectations, setting developmental goals, establishing a learning culture, and tracking the effects of organizational change. Detailed guidelines show how 360-degree feedback can be designed to maximize employee involvement, self-determination, and commitment. Filled with case examples and a full complement of instructive instruments.

Hardcover   408 pages   Item #F093 $42.95

"This wonderfully useful guide to leadership development will prove an invaluable resource to anyone interested in growing the talent of their organizations."
—Jay A. Conger, professor, USC, and author of *Learning to Lead*

The Center for Creative Leadership
Handbook of Leadership Development
Cynthia D. McCauley, Russ S. Moxley, Ellen Van Velsor, Editors

In one comprehensive volume, the Center for Creative Leadership distills its philosophy, findings, and methodologies into a practical resource that sets a new standard in the field. Filled with proven techniques and detailed instructions for designing and enabling the most effective leadership development programs possible—including six developed by CCL itself—this is the ultimate professional guide from one of the most prestigious organization in the field.

Hardcover   480 pages   Item #F116 $65.00

"At last, a practical, quick, direct, and easy-to-use tool that helps individuals flex their learning muscles! I'll use the Learning Tactics Inventory (LTI) in my consulting practice right away."
—Beverly Kaye, author, *Up Is Not the Only Way*

Learning Tactics Inventory
Facilitator's Guide & Participant Workbook
Maxine Dalton

Developed by CCL, the *Learning Tactics Inventory (LTI)* gives you everything you need to conduct a two- to four-hour workshop that dramatically enhances participants' ability to learn by showing each individual how he or she learns best and how each can adopt new learning strategies accordingly. The *Inventory* is used by workshop participants to profile their individual learning behaviors. The *Participant Workbook* is used to score and interpret results. The *Facilitator's Guide*, which includes a sample copy of the *Participant Workbook* and the *Inventory*, details all key workshop procedures—including setup, administration, and follow-up—and comes with reproducible overhead and handout masters. You'll need one *Inventory* and *Workbook* per participant, available at bulk discounts.

LTI Inventory within Participant Workbook paperback   48 pages
Item #G515 $12.95
LTI Facilitator's Guide [includes sample Workbook] paperback   56 pages   Item #G514 $24.95

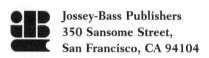